A Grundtvig Anthology

A GRUNDTVIG ANTHOLOGY

SELECTIONS FROM THE WRITINGS
OF
N. F. S. GRUNDTVIG
(1783-1872)

Translated by
Edward Broadbridge and Niels Lyhne Jensen

Edited, annotated and introduced by
Niels Lyhne Jensen, William Michelsen, Gustav Albeck,
Hellmut Toftdahl, Chr. Thodberg

GENERAL EDITOR: NIELS LYHNE JENSEN

James Clarke & Co
Cambridge

Centrum
Denmark

A Grundtvig Anthology

Selections from the writings of
N. F. S. Grundtvig (1783-1872)
© Centrum 1984
Translated by Edward Broadbridge
and Niels Lyhne Jensen
General editor: Niels Lyhne Jensen
Cover design: Inga-Britt Liljeroth
Illustration: Grundtvig, 1831,
painting by C. A. Jensen
(Ny Carlsberg Glyptotek)
Printed in Denmark 1984

ISBN 0-227-67885-0 (U.K.)
ISBN 87-583-0158-5 (Denmark)

Published by:
James Clarke & Co
7 All Saints' Passage
Cambridge CB2 3LS
England

Centrum
Grøndalsvej 3
8260 Viby
Denmark

An anthology of the writings of N. F. S. Grundtvig was planned by a committee set up by the Grundtvig Society. Its commission was to produce an anthology of Grundtvig's writings in English translation which would acquaint the foreign student with Grundtvig's ideas through his own words, thus supplementing the various monographs on his work in English. The selections include extracts from his historical, educational, theological, devotional and poetical work. The individual chapters are provided with special introductions. Dr. phil. William Michelsen of Aarhus University has written about the texts in chapter III and IV, Professor dr. phil. Gustav Albeck of Aarhus University has introduced chapter V, Hellmut Toftdahl, mag. art., chapter VI, Professor dr. phil. Chr. Thodberg of Aarhus University chapter VII, and Niels Lyhne Jensen, cand. mag., M. A., of Aarhus University chapter VIII. The texts were translated by Edward Broadbridge, B. A., and the Editor who has also written a general introduction and annotated the texts.

The Editor is grateful to The Fortress Press for permission to print the translations of two poems pp. 191-192, to the American-Scandinavian Foundation for permission to print the translation of the poem on p. 193, and to Mrs. Hilda Egglishaw for permission to use the translation by the late John Jepson Egglishaw on p. 188.

The Grundtvig Society records its gratitude to Forskningsfonden, Aarhus University for a grant towards translation fees and to Jyllands-Postens Fond for a generous donation making it possible to get the book printed for the Bicentenary of N. F. S. Grundtvig's birth.

Niels Lyhne Jensen
General Editor

Chr. Thodberg
President
The Grundtvig Society

Table of Contents

I   Biographical Table   9

II   Introduction   13

III   From Grundtvig's Introduction
to Norse Mythology 1832   31

IV   The School for Life   63

V   Selections from Within Living Memory   85

VI   Selections from Elementary
Christian Teachings   125

VII   Sermons   161

VIII   Poetry   183

I

Biographical table

Nikolaj Frederik Severin Grundtvig
1783-1872

1783	Born at Udby Parsonage, Zealand, on 8th September as the third and youngest son of Johan Ottosen Grundtvig (1734–1813) and wife Cathrine Marie, née Bang (1748–1822).
1792	G. is farmed out for tuition at a parsonage at Thyregod, Jutland.
1798	After First Communion G. enters the grammar school at Aarhus, Jutland.
1800	Matriculates at the University of Copenhagen.
1803	G. passes the degree of divinity with a first-class mark on 25th October.
1803–1804	G.'s first attempts as a writer and his introduction to Old Norse language and literature.
1805–1808	Tutor at the Manor of Egeløkke, Langeland.
1808–1810	Works as a writer and schoolmaster in Copenhagen.
1810	After his probationary sermon G. enters a religious crises ending in mental collapse.
1811–1812	Curate to his father at Udby.
1813–1821	Works as a writer and translator in Copenhagen.
1818	Marries Elisabeth (Lise) Blicher (1787–1851).
1821	Appointed to the living of the parish of Præstø, Zealand.
1822–1826	Transfers to the pulpit of the Church of our Saviour, Copenhagen.
1825	G.'s "discovery" of a foundation of Christianity in the Apostles' Creed at Baptism and his attack on liberal scripture theology in "The Rejoinder of the Church".
1826	Resigns from his living in May. Loses law-suit for libel on 30th October with the consequence that G. is subjected to censorship until 1837.
1829–1831	During three summers G. visits England with the aim of studying Anglo-Saxon manuscripts.

1832	The introduction to the second edition of G.'s Norse Mythology marks a significant new departure in his views about Christianity, human life and secular culture.
1838	G. outlines his ideas about "the living word" and education of the people in residential schools in "The School for Life".
1839	Receives appointment as Pastor of Vartov Hospital, Copenhagen, in which post G. remains to the end of his life.
1843	Last visit to England.
1844	G. succumbs to a servere depression from which he emerges with renewed spiritual and physical strength.
1848–1849	Member of the Constituent Assembly working out a democratic constitution for Denmark, but abstains in the vote on the reform bill.
1851	Marries Ane Marie Elise Toft, née Carlsen (1813–1854) after the death of his first wife.
1853	Member of Parliament (the Lower House, the Folketing).
1854–1858	Member of Parliament (the Lower House, the Folketing).
1858	Marries his third wife Asta Tugendreich Adelheid Reedtz, née Krag-Juel-Vind-Frijs (1826–1890).
1861	Is given title and rank of Bishop in recognition of G.'s contribution to the life of the Danish Church.
1866	Member of Parliament (The Upper House, the Landsting).
1867	An outbreak of G.'s mental illness becomes evident during the service on Palm Sunday.
1872	Dies on 2. September after preaching his last sermon the previous day. Buried on 11th September and laid to rest in the grave vault of the family of his second wife at Gammel Køgegaard, Zealand.

II

Introduction

Nikolaj Frederik Severin Grundtvig (1783-1872) takes up a position in the life and culture of Denmark which is unique. He is one of the most original poets in the language, and his best work, to be found in the hymns he wrote for the Danish Lutheran Church, has also made his poetry perhaps the best loved of alle literary works in Danish. Furthermore, his view of Christianity and its relation to secular culture has left an indelible mark on the life of Danish society in all its aspects from church life and education to political affairs and economic activities. Grundtvig also made memorable contributions to Anglo-Saxon philology and to the study of mythology and history. Finally his personal development, as it is known to us through his diaries, poetry, sermons and essays, is in itself a fascinating saga about the way an unusual and powerful personality relates and reacts to the events and ideas of the 19th century and constantly struggles to understand the mystery of man and his destiny in history.

Grundtvig was born at the parsonage of Udby in South Zealand on 8th September 1783. He came into the world when the Kingdom of Denmark had enjoyed a long span of peace, and when trade and commerce with the Far East and the West Indies brought a hitherto unknown prosperity to the middle classes, while some measure of reform to relieve the social oppression and economic misery of the peasantry was inaugured. Grundtvig's father was a gentle learned clergyman who held to a pietist orthodoxy at a time when the Danish Church was dominated by theological Rationalism. Both Grundtvig's parents came from families of clerics and civil servants. His strong-minded mother belonged to a kin that traced its ancestry back to a renowned noble family of the Danish middle ages. Grundtvig was the youngest of four children and was brought up with a sister, one year his senior. They were looked after by an old nurse-maid whose store of popular beliefs and legends made a deep impression on the child. At an astonishingly early age

Grundtvig browsed over historical chronicles in his father's library. Among his earliest recollections is the announcement of the prelude to the French Revolution by the radical local schoolmaster.

At the age of nine Grundtvig was farmed out with his father's former curate at the parsonage of Thyregod, Jutland. The pastor offered board and tuition to sons of the clergy whom he prepared for the grammar school. Grundtvig was well and humanely taught and always remembered his kind and open-minded tutor with affection. The dark heathlands around Thyregod, so different from the lush rolling scenery of his native region, made a lasting impression on the boy, as did the ways and speech of the Jutish peasants.

After First Communion in 1798 Grundtvig was admitted to the senior form of the grammar school at Aarhus, Jutland. Later in his life he described his school years as a dreadful stultifying grind mainly devoted to the classics, Hebrew and scripture. On his own Grundtvig read history.

Grundtvig matriculated at the University of Copenhagen in 1800 as a student of divinity, to which field of study, on his own admission, he devoted himself with little diligence and faith. He soon exchanged the stern orthodoxy in which he had been brought up for the theological Rationalism of the day. In spite of modest means Grundtvig took part in the usual undergraduate life: amateur acting, card-playing, pipe-smoking and drinking, but also found time for reading modern literature and history. Thanks to an energetic spurt of swotting before his finals he nonetheless passed his degree exams with a first-class mark. As a graduate he went deeper into historical and literary studies while continuing the versifying and writing he had begun at an earlier date. He tried his hand unsuccesfully at various genres from comic verse and comedy to novellas with Norse themes and a Sternean novel. The career of a writer seems to have been his ambition rather than that of the pulpit. During this time his interest in Norse literature led him to the study of the Old Norse Language.

In 1805 the state of his finances made him accept a position as a tutor with a land-owning family at the Manor of Egeløkke in the island of Langeland in the Baltic. He was to teach a seven-year old boy, a task he pursued with extraordinary energy and seriousness. It was not easy for the somewhat uncouth young academic to adapt to the polite ways of the gentry, but after a while he engaged himself in the life of the local community, preaching in the Church and taking the initiative in founding a reading society.

The most important event of his island existence was, however, that from the very first day he fell in love with the beautiful mistress of the Manor, Mrs Constance de Steensen Leth, his senior by six years. This unhappy and futureless passion drove him to the edge of despair and he nearly succumbed from the conflict between his raging desire and his strong moral sense, but his sufferings also roused him to a hitherto unknown self-awareness and released enormous spiritual and intellectual energies within him. Now he grasped the Romantics' view of the divinity of Nature and their idea of poetry as a revelation of the eternal to which he had been introduced by his kinsman, the philosopher Henrik Steffens, though without comprehending his words. He absorbed himself in romantic philosophy and poetry, the works of Schelling and Fichte and the poetry of Novalis and Oehlenschlaeger. He also read Goethe and Schiller as well as the poet, who was to become a life-long inspiration, William Shakespeare. Only for a time, however, did the romantic notion of the harmonization of all polarities by an intuitive vision satisfy him. Grundtvig followed another romantic lead as he sought for the divine universal spirit in the remote past, in ancient Scandinavian history and Norse mythology. He entered a stage in his development which he later with reference to the Norse name of the ancient gods called his asamania. Grundtvig saw in the myths of the North a reflection of the Eternal and an expression of the moral values and understanding of life of the Norsemen and rejected with scorn the current interpretation of myths as symbolic representations of natural phenomena. In essays on the Edda and the Norse pantheon and in a book, his "Norse Mythology" (1808) Grundtvig makes an original contribution to mythological scholarship as he selects the lays of the Edda as primary sources for our knowledge of Norse religion. In keeping with romantic thought he presents a unified vision of the myths. He sees them as a drama with a moral trend: the divine life of the gods is flawed by sensuality, breach of faith and murder all of which launches the events leading to Ragnarok, the end of the world, when the gods perish in a heroic battle against the giants, the forces of evil. The epilogue with the rebirth of the gods in evergreen plains to immortal life Grundtvig takes as a symbol both of religious hope and of national rebirth after the humiliation Denmark had suffered in the wars with England.

Grundtvig had by then become the ardent patriot he was to remain for the rest of his life.

By way of his asamania, during which for a time he thought of Scandinavian paganism as a manifestation of the Divine equal with Christianity, Grundtvig reverted to the Lutheran faith in which he had been raised. His development is evident in the two cycles of dramatic scenes with themes from Norse mythology and the heroic legends found in the Edda, which represent the most ambitious fruit of his early creativity as a poet. By 1808 Grundtvig had returned to Copenhagen where he immersed himself in historical studies while making a living as a publicist and a schoolmaster. He now seemed set upon an academic career.

Grundtvig gave expression to his orthodox Christian standpoint and his judgment of the Rationalist clergy of the day in his probationary sermon in 1810, which, when he had it printed, earned him a rebuke from the University Senate. Afterwards he turned the accusation of failing faith against himself, which threw him into a religious crisis. This in connection with over-work and Grundtvig's inbred manio-depressive disposition produced a mental collapse verging on insanity. On recovering he humbly accepted to become curate to his ailing father at Udby, and for two years with his wonted zeal Grundtvig devoted himself to preaching and pastoral work. In 1812 he worked up his notes for his teaching of history into a Short Summary of a World Chronicle. In his preface Grundtvig states it as his plan to write a theodicy of history, that is, he will show the birth of Christ as the central event in history and, by showing God's finger in the progress of mankind, prove the truth of Christianity through history. He also wants his book to serve as mirror to the ungodly present in Denmark and to call for Christian reform both in the Church and in national life. In spite of the unifying idea for his work, which Romanticism had taught him, Grundtvig does not succeed in carrying out his plan. Early history is very cursorily dealt with while his treatment of the period from the Reformation to the present day gives the main emphasis to the eighteenth century and the most recent times. The work, which is perhaps better described as a history of ideas than a general history, shows Grundtvig's impressive reading in European history and thought, but it is flawed by the author's often coarsely polemical dismissal of the thinkers and writers of the Age of Reason in France. His regained Christian orthodoxy makes him also turn on his former Romantic idols, particular Schelling, whose philosophy of Nature is denounced as a godless naturalism. Grundtvig's world chronicle is, however, not to be read as an account of history, but as an example of how Grundtvig makes use of history to explore and clarify his view of existence. This also holds true of the revisions of the World Chronicle he made in 1814 and 1817. In the latter, without abandoning the christocentric view of history, Grundtvig recognizes that historical scholarship must be based on documented knowledge.

The World Chronicle of 1812, which went against the grain of all contemporary historical writing, gave occasion for the first of the many polemical bouts in which Grundtvig was involved during his lifetime. Grundtvig's condemnation of Schelling particularly outraged Hans Christian Oersted, the eminent physicist, who became Grundtvig's main adversary. This quarrel, combined with other writings and speeches in which Grundtvig passed judgment on the Church and the Nation, earned him a reputation as a turbulent priest and lost him his prospects of an academic career, just as it isolated him from the intellectual establishment of the day. As he did not want to be considered a fanatic and, besides was disappointed in the response to his preaching, Grundtvig laid down the cloth in 1815.

The years from 1815 to 1821 he has himself described as his historical period. In a periodical "Dannevirke," which he filled up singlehanded, he published translations of documents about national history, literary and historical essays and poems with historical and religious themes, all with the aim of promoting a revival of faith and a regeneration of national life. His main contribution in this respect is, however, his translations of the two principal literary moments of the Scandinavian middle ages, Saxo's *Gesta Danorum* and Snorri Sturluson's *Heimskringla*, the history of the Kings of medieval Norway. In his attempt to make these works attractive to the common reader Grundtvig adopts a popular style drawing on popular saws and proverbs as well as dialect vocabulary. An original achievement! which hardly succeeded in its aim to reach the people. In addition to these impressive philological feats Grundtvig did a translation of Beowulf, the original text of which had recently been published in Copenhagen for the first time.

The toil of his formidable translation tasks, which sequestered him in his study, had in the long run a deadening effect on him, and it was with some relief that he accepted a living at Præstø, Zealand in 1821, from which he moved on to the pulpit of the Church of Our Saviour in Copenhagen the following year.

Yet, he was still in the doldrums. He had misgivings about the usefulness of his historical writings for a national awakening, and the apology for Christianity he tried to write failed to satisfy him. An important inspiration from these years is, however, his reading of Irenæus's "Against the Heretics", which Grundtvig translated. Irenæus's emphasis on man as God's creation redeemed by Christ and his teaching about God's essence as life and love became of the greatest importance to the new view of Christianity that dawned on him. In the Advent Season of 1823 the ferment of his mind came to fruition: he was filled with a feeling of having become alive in every sense, as a believer, as a poet and as a national reformer. This whole process he has described in a long poem where he uses a myth, drawn from Saxo, as a foil for describing his own development, a heroic quest through a Nordic underworld of cold and shadows which ends when, led by a woman both personifying Denmark and life, he reaches the ice wall of death where, however, he receives a token of immortality from the other side. The preface of the poem contains a terse formulation of the way he now sees his task as a poet and as an educator of the nation: he is "to revive the Norse heroic spirit to Christian deeds along lines suitable to the needs and terms of the present day."

The elation and vitality, felt at the time, also contributed to a clarification of Grundtvig's view of Christianity. He came to realize that the word of God to man was not primarily the text of the Bible, but the audible word of God spoken at baptism and communion. It has been heard in the Church from the beginning, a living word, in which the Lord himself was present as he was in the sacraments. Upon this "matchless discovery" Grundtvig founds his historico-ecclesiastical view of Christianity which sets an epoch in the history of the Danish Church. In a sermon given on 31st July 1825 he proclaims his new position for the first time.

Grundtvig now felt that he was well armed against the modern sciptural criticism that had disquieted him. In August of the same year a young theologian and Bible scholar Professor H. N. Clausen published a book on "The Constitution of Catholicism and Protestantism. Doctrine and Ritual". Here he defines the Church as a "community for the promotion of general religiosity" and confirms that Holy Writ remains the foundation of faith, albeit as it is currently checked and corrected by biblical scholars. On reading this, Grundtvig erupted. In a pamphlet, stirring up much attention, "The Rejoinder of the Church", he denounces Clausen's teachings on all counts. His concept of the Church is a "castle in the air" and his attitude to the Bible contradictory. Instead Grundtvig points to his own historico-ecclesiastical view as an irrefutable foundation of Christian faith. In violent terms he brands Clausen's position as false and challenges him either to retract or lay down his office as a teacher and drop the name of a Christian.

To Grundtvig's chagrin his opponent did not join in a debate but brought a law-suit for libel. In October 1826 the findings of the court went against Grundtvig, he was made to pay a fine and had censorship imposed on him, under which he remained until 1837. Some months previously Grundtvig had tendered his resignation from the pulpit once again. The immediate occasion for this was the church authorities' refusal to allow him to use some hymns he had written commemorating the thousandth anniversary for the first Christian mission to Denmark in the service for Whitsunday.

Though both hurt and subdued over the outcome of this clash with the theological establishment, Grundtvig was heartened to find that he had followers both among the clergy and the laity in his struggle. In a periodical founded by two of his academic disciples he wrote two articles substantiating his theological position. He also penned a longish essay "On the Freedom of Religion", which was suppressed by the authorities. In these years he considered the idea of founding a free church and, in 1831 even prepared a petition to the King for permission to establish one. He also toyed with the idea of emigrating to Norway or England where he hoped to find freer conditions under which to live and work.

In 1828 he returned to his interest in the heroic past and obtained a grant from the King to go to England to study and copy Anglo-Saxon manuscripts, which he believed contained the earliest sources for Scandinavian history and literature.

During the summers of 1829, 1830 and 1831 Grundtvig visited England and did unearth and copy Anglo-Saxon manuscripts that had hitherto been neglected and ignored. Though nothing came of his plans to publish them, Grundtvig is still a pioneer of Anglo-Saxon scholarship by drawing the attention of English scholars to their cultural heritage. But Grundtvig's main benefit was not to be in the field of learning. It was the life of the present day in England that became his main interest. To be true, at first England was a disappointment to him, he found the English dull and inhospitable, he had difficulty with the language, and the Anglican Church struck him as entirely lifeless. Also his impression of Henry Irving and his preaching, about which he had had some expectations, proved entirely negative. Gradually, however, he was struck by the witality of the English. The activity and enterprise of England in the heyday of industrialism struck him as a contrast to the inertia of his native land. It appeared to him that it was the Norse spirit of yore that manifested itself in the bustling factory halls, though he also had an eye for the dark side to the new industry, just as he found little to admire in the English parliamentary system. The residential colleges of Oxford and Cambridge, where he spent some time, on the other hand, greatly appealed to him in spite of the classical learning dominating them. He thought the colleges ideal forums for the exchange of ideas and felt very much in his element when he was invited to high tables.

These impressions, combined with the deep personal inspiration he drew from the meeting with the beautiful and brilliant Clara Bolton, the friend of Disraeli, was to call forth significant changes in his views on all scores in the years following immediately after.

When in 1832 Grundtvig was bringing out a second edition of his "Norse Mythology", he uses the introduction to the totally revised work to give an outline of the reorientation of his general outlook. In his discussion of universal-historical learning he expresses his hopes for a new life-inspiring knowledge when the soul-destroying classical scholarship has been cast overboard as the dead heritage of Roman and Italian erudition it is. What Grundtvig now wants to see realized is a learning and culture, which draw on the heroic spirit of Norse legends and the genius inherent in Greek myths, and are combined with a "Mosaic-Christian" way of thinking. The distinction Grundtvig here explicitly makes between way of thinking and faith is crucial. A Mosaic-Christian way of thinking recognizes that Christianity gave to the thought and culture of the world of nations a universal human character that was not known before. It also accepts man as being essentially distinct from dumb creatures, a synthesis of dust and clay, which is conscious of its spiritual nature and to itself is a wonderful mystery. With all who can agree on this view of history and man Grundtvig is prepared to cooperate, irrespective of their attitude to the central doctrines of Christian faith, in working out a programme for education, aimed at life and taught predominantly through the medium of the living word. The secular aim of his educational ideas now is also tersely expressed in a poem from 1837 with the much quoted line: "A human being first, a Christian later. That is the order of nature". A fundamental condition of all spiritual endeavour is finally freedom. Grundtvig expresses this in the introductory rhymed greetings to the Norse kinsmen with the equally famous words: "Freedom for Loki as well as for Thor!" That is freedom both for the principles Grundtvig himself embraced and for those he fought against.

The complex of ideas here outlined represents the decisive clarification of Grundtvig's views. He has reached the position from which at the age of fifty he is to begin a new and major epoch in his career as a poet, a churchman, an educationist and a politician.

In the years following immediately after 1832 Grundtvig's creative energy is at its highest. In continuation of his mythology he published a handbook of world history in three volumes 1833, 1836 and 1843. Gone is here the christocentric view of history. In his account of the development of the major nations he wishes to show how they fulfill their role in world history in accordance with their innate siprit as it is manifest in their respective mythologies. His emphasis is on his favourites, the Hebrews, the Greeks, the Anglo-Saxons and the Norsemen whom he sees as the bearers of the progress of mankind while the Romans and the French only stood in its way. Grundtvig predicts that in the modern age the world historical task of the North – i.e. Scandinavia and Britain – will be to further the cause of the mother tongue, the freedom of conscience and the right of people to their native language. Grundtvig's Herderean interpretation of history does not satisfy scholarly demands, its aim is educational and Grundtvig makes it a vehichle for the liberal ideas he has now reached. The handbook of world history remained incomplete, it went no further than 1800, but Grundtvig dealt with the modern history of Europe in his celebrated course of lectures "Within Living Memory" delivered in 1838.

In these talks Grundtvig realized for the first time with success his idea of the living word as a means of communication in contrast to the deadening effect of all book learning. The very concept of the living word is central to the series of essays on education from the Thirties where he develops his seminal ideas about education for life offered to the entire young generation and not only to those set on an academic or professional career. The principal work is "The School for Life" 1838.

Grundtvig's engagement in the life of his times is evident from his membership of the constituent assembly formed in 1848 with the purpose of drafting a proposal for a democratic constitution for Denmark. Grundtvig had previously been no admirer of parliamentary democracy as is clear from his rejection of the English political system in 1838, as well as from the falsely idyllic picture of the absolute monarchy in Denmark he long clung to. When it came to a vote in the assembly on the constitution bill, Grundtvig abstained. He thought the proposal smacked too much of its Belgian and French models and found it too difficult to change. When the constitution was adopted, Grundtvig loyally accepted it. As a politician he remained an independent, but vigorously championed the causes of education and ecclesiastical freedom. In 1866, at the age of eighty-three he stood for the Upper House to protest, to no avail, against the restriction of the general franchise that was introduced with a new constitutional reform.

With all his public activities Grundtvig was first and last a poet and a preacher. In 1837 he published "A Hymnary for the Danish Church" which was supplemented by another heavy volume in 1870. In addition to those there printed, there are numerous others. Including translations the hymns number some 1400, all of which have now been published in five volumes.

As a translator Grundtvig does not faithfully render the meaning of the originals, he rather takes off from their wording and theme to express his own poetic idea. He finds his models in a number of languages: Greek, Latin, Anglo-Saxon, English and German. In the same way he reworks old Danish hymns, sometimes in a striking way changing them from penitentiary laments over the world and the wretchedness of man to songs of praise in creation and Christian life in this world. The first hymns by Grundtvig entered the Danish hymn-book in 1855. In the version now in use he dominates with some 200 titles out of a total of 700.

Grundtvig's hymns are as a rule not personal, but interprets the situation of the congregation in worship. He has covered all the occasions of the ecclesiastical year and Christian life as well as the sacraments, baptism and communion. Foremost among his hymns are perhaps those written for Whitsunday which to Grundtvig's logos theology must rank as the principal holy season.

In his hymns as in all his poetry Grundtvig employs a complex imagery drawn from the Bible and from Norse mythology and Danish folk beliefs. Grundtvig's imagination and thought function in terms of images and symbols that relate to a coherent system, which makes his poetry only fully understandable to those who are familiar with a reasonable portion of his work. Conspicuous in his style is the use of antitheses such as life and death, summer and winter, night and day, which are all pregnant with connotations lent to them by Grundtvig's symbolic universe. That is also true of the pairs of colours, red and white, black and golden, and of his frequent references to phenomena of light and radiance. Grundtvig's predominantly substantival language is made even more compact by his predeliction for compound nouns. He also writes with a keen sense of the root meaning of words, and he is an irrepressible punner. As a truly original poet Grundtvig is gifted with a grandiose lack of conventional taste, as he draws his vocabulary from archaic sources, popular saws and dialect. The landscape of his hymns is Danish. In those for Christmas the bringing of the good tidings may take place on a frosty winter's night when the ground is covered with snow. Likewise, the pentecostal miracle coalesces with the greening and flowering of the sunny Zealand scenery at Whitsuntide. This reflects how Grundtvig dramatically relives in his worship the great moments of Christian faith.

Beside his hymns Grundtvig wrote a number of devotional songs and ballads with themes from the Bible where he sometimes models himself on popular broadsides. Parallel to the Christian poetry are the songs written in praise of the fatherland. Many of these were written for use in the people's high schools which is also true of the many narrative poems on historical themes. The majority of these deals with the Danish past, but there are others devoted to the great figures of world history as for example the magnificent long poem about Christopher Columbus.

A great many poems are written for special occasions and addressed to friends and members of Grundtvig's family. Most of these are now of purely historical interest, but a few are of great poetic merit as for instance the "Open Letter to my Children" (1838), the obituary poem for Henrik Steffens (1845) and the poem "For Klara" addressed to Clara Bolton (1844).

As a preacher Grundtvig was active from his early twenties to the day before his death as a near nonagenarian. Some 3000 sermons are registered in the Grundtvig archives in the Royal Library of Copenhagen.

In Grundtvig's preaching before 1832 he speaks as a chastiser of the Lutheran Church and as a rouser of a morally degenerate nation. His outlook on life is that of the dark penitentiary Lutheran faith he had inherited from his fathers. In line with this is the solemn and prophetic manner of his sermons. In the 1830 there is a significant change. Grundtvig no longer lays claim to any missionary role, and his style is less rhetorical and more relaxed. The themes of his preaching now tend to be his historico-ecclesiastical view and the sacraments. He also stresses the distinction between the State Church as merely a civic establishment and the Living Church of true believers. The sermons also register Grundtvig's reactions to the issues of the day. In the 1850es it is evident how Grundtvig from the pulpit tried to reply to Kierkegaard's violent attacks on the Church and its clergy, an onslaught that was not least aimed at himself.

When Grundtvig stepped forward as a man with a religious and national mission in the second decade of the 19th century, he was an isolated figure whom the literary and academic establishment eyed with distaste and ridicule. In the Twenties a small flock forgathered round his pulpit. It abandoned him, to be true, after his significant metamorphosis in 1832, but a new following of young theologians and laity rallied round him. When in 1839 he had his own pulpit again in Vartov Hospital, the small chapel there became a centre of a vigorous congregational life where communion and the singing of hymns by Grundtvig became the dominant element of the service rather than the sermon. From Vartov a movement spread that in the Forties became nationwide. Grundtvig's ideas about adult education were realized at the people's high school founded at Roedding in North Schleswig in 1844, and soon after others were established. None of the schools developed quite the way Grundtvig wanted, which may explain why, apart from one, he never visited any of them. Though Grundtvig was the central figure of a popular movement that was active in the Church, education and politics, he never became an organizer or leader of a party. Grundtvig, however, was looked upon by his followers as their spiritual head, and when after his third marriage he was able to afford a largish house and household, his home at Store Tuborg north of the capital on the road to Elsinore became a mekka for Grundtvigians who came to obtain guidance or simply to get inspiration from the presence of the great old man.

After fifty Grundtvig seems a happier, more humorous and outward-going personality than he had been earlier on. Yet, his personal life was not without shadows. His first marriage was far from happy during its last years, and in 1844 he was afflicted with mental illness due to over-work and his innate manio-depressive disposition. Grundtvig was, however, able to recover with unimpaired mental faculties and renewed energy. The death of his second wife after a short, but very happy married life was a severe blow to him, but he rose again, and in his third marriage fathered a daughter at the age of 75. In 1867 after his last stand as a politician he once again lapsed into mental illness which became evident during mass on Palm-Sunday. But even at this advanced age Grundtvig recovered and, though physically frail, went on writing and preaching.

Edmund Gosse, the English poet and critic, has recorded the following impression of Grundtvig at Vartov during the last year of his life in 1872:

We arrived, however, so far as seeing the great man was concerned, in most ample time at the little Workhouse Church, opposite the trees and still waters of the western ramparts. We found seats with difficulty, the chapel being crowded with communicants, doubtless attracted by a rumour that this would be the last time that the aged prophet would address his disciples. After sitting more than half an hour, surrounded by strange, fanatic faces, and women who swung themselves backward and forward in silent prayer, the word was passed round that the Bishop would probably be unable to come. The congregation began to sing hymns of his composition in a loud, quick, staccato manner invented by the poet, which was very little like the slow singing in the State churches. Suddenly, and when we had given up all hope, there entered from the vestry and walked rapidly to the altar a personage who seemed to me the oldest human being I had ever seen. Instantly an absolute silence prevailed throughout the church, and then there rose a sound as though some one were talking in the cellar below our feet. It was the Bishop praying aloud at the altar, and then he turned and addressed the communicants in the same dull, veiled voice. He wandered down among the ecstatic worshippers, and stood close at my side for a moment, while he laid his hands on a girl's head, so that I saw his face to perfection. For a man of ninety, he could not be called infirm; his gestures were rapid and his step steady. But the attention was riveted on his appearance of excessive age. He looked like a troll from some cave in Norway; he might have been centuries old.

From the vast orb of his bald head, very long strings of silky hair fell over his shoulders and mingled with a long and loose white beard. His eyes flamed under very beetling brows, and they were the only part of his face that seemed alive, for he spoke without moving his lips. His features were still shapely, but colourless and dry, and as the draught from an open door caught them, the silken hairs were blown across his face like a thin curtain. While he perambulated the church with these stiff gestures and ventriloquist murmurings, his disciples fell on their knees behind him, stroking the skirts of his robe, touching the heels of his shoes. Finally, he ascended the pulpit and began to preach; in his dead voice he warned us to beware of false spirits, and to try every spirit whether it be of God. He laboured extremely with his speech, becoming slower and huskier, with longer pauses between the words like a clock that is running down. He looked supernatural, but hardly Christian. If, in the body of the church, he had reminded me of a troll, in the pulpit he looked more like some belated Druid, who had survived from Mona and could not die.

Edmund Gosse: *Two Visits to Denmark* (1911) p. 85-87.

About a month later on 1st September 1872 Grundtvig celebrated mass as usual. The following day he died quietly sitting in his armchair. The funeral took place on 11th September, and his followers came from afar in the Kingdom and Norway to join the thousands that walked in the funeral procession. Thus his last journey turned into a powerful manifestation of the strength and vitality of the movement among the Danish people Grundtvig had inspired.

To give a fair impression of Grundtvig's personality, ideas and achievement within a short space is hardly feasible. There is the risk of attaching to him labels which, when speaking of a poet and spiritual leader of the nineteenth century, lie near at hand, but in Grundtvig's case still would be misleading. Grundtvig is greatly indebted to the romantic movement, yet he is no romantic. He owes little or nothing to Schleiermacher's romantic theology and does not in his maturity share the romantics' idealist conception of man. Though no one has declared his love of his fatherland with greater warmth than Grundtvig, he is no traditional nationalist. He only recognised that man was necessarily born into a particular nation and to a particular language and would grasp and understand life in this mould and in this tongue. But love of the fatherland to Grundtvig certainly did not mean any aggressive or expansionist nationalism of the German type, which he rightly saw as a danger. Grundtvig greatly emphasised the cultural unity of the Scandinavian nations, but he would have no truck with the political Pan-Scandinavianism which was a strong movement among young academic liberals in the Forties and Fifties. Nor has his enthusiasm for Scandinavian myths any similarity with the sinister Teutonic gibberish Wagner and others made of it in the second half of the century. Closely allied with Grundtvig's love of his fatherland is his deep interest in the traditional life and culture of the people. For the values he found here he uses the Danish word "folkelig", which it is near impossible to translate into English. In some contexts it is synonymous with national, but not in all. It may refer to folkways and narratives and poems handed down by oral tradition, but not exclusively. It certainly does not mean popular in the sense of vulgarized knowledge processed for mass consumption. "Folkelig" refers to a cultural and social life which draws from the traditions and values shared by all the people, and in which they actively participate. The term might also be opposed to academic in the sense that Grundtvig wanted to give an education to the people based on Danish language, literature and history which would enrich the personal life of the individual, but also enable him to engage himself in public life with self-reliance and dignity. Finally it must be mentioned that Grundtvig became a great champion of freedom. It meant to him spiritual freedom, freedom of speech and freedom of conscience. It is fine to see how as he grew older he attached greater and greater importance to the idea of liberty in public life.

If one were to describe Grundtvig by one word, it would be the term "vitalist". Life is to him the supreme value in every sphere. In his diary from Langeland he writes when he had fallen in love: "There is in me a desire for life even stronger than my desire for love." Just as death to Grundtvig does not mean merely physical death but a feeling of existence as barren and negative, in the same way "to live" is not just being but to be in contact with strength, warmth and love. Hence the jubilation with which he records in 1824 that he has become alive again. It is life that strikes him as the outstanding quality of the work of the pagan Shakespeare, and it is the overwhelming impression of vitality and action that makes him admire England and the English. When pressed by the German Hegelian theologian Marheinecke to state his position on the distinction between being and thought, Grundtvig replied: "My antithesis is life and death." In his greatest poem "The Land of the Living", printed p. 188 f., Grundtvig in the concluding lines makes life synonymous with the Godhead: "My land, says Life, is on earth and above, my Kingdom of love."

Joy of life, openness and freedom are qualities that mark the movements in church life, education, cooperative societies and politics, associated with Grundtvig, which from the second half of the nineteenth century make such a significant impact on Danish society. To be true, they were not the work of Grundtvig, but arose out of the social and economic conditions of the time. But his ideas undoubtedly lent to their members among the agrarian lower middle classes a distinct life style, an elan and richness of their community life, which is unique. With the social and economic transformation of Denmark in this century the influence of Grundtvig on Danish society is fading, but it is still there, and of how many great poets could it be said that what they saw and dreamt is still felt in society at large in the bicentenary of their birth.

Niels Lyhne Jensen

III

From Grundtvig's
Introduction to Norse Mythology
1832

Universal-historical learning is part I of Grundtvig's introduction to his comprehensive monograph on Norse mythology (1832), which became the book of reference for all the lectures given at Grundtvigian folk high schools in the 19th century. In addition the present part of the introduction may be said to contain Grundtvig's ideas about culture. As an alternative to classical learning and the erudition of the Italian Renaissance Grundtvig puts forward his ideas for a Nordic renaissance in agreement with the biblical, i.e. Mosaic-Christian view of man and his history. The essay sets an epoch in Grundtvig's work as from now on and to his death in 1872 he combines his Christian view of history and man with the demand for freedom of belief as well as knowledge, that is, in religion and learning, whereas before 1832 he considered it his duty as a Christian priest (since 1810) to preach Christianity in anything he spoke and wrote.

In his monograph he regards Norse mythology as a symbolic representation of the view of life of the Norsemen as it was immediately before they came into contact with Christianity, and in his account he draws not only on Icelandic sources but also on Beowulf and the Danish lay of Bjarki, only preserved in Latin translation in Saxo's legendary history, which is also used. The inclusion of the latter sources makes the book different from Grundtvig's short mythology of 1808, with which it has the title in common.

An important feature of the present text is that it makes a clear distinction between faith and way of thinking. The Christian way of thinking about human life was unconditionally shared by Grundtvig and the majority of those who had been his opponents: Man is created with a divine purpose, although early in his history he had strayed from it. It is within his power to find his way back to the right path? Grundtvig claims that man is incapable thereof, even with Christ as his model. He believes that only God in baptism and communion has power to do so. Grundtvig's particular standpoint did not prevent him from working together with people who did not agree with his belief. He made it an explicit condition, however, that they accepted his aforementioned way of thinking while insisting on the freedom of any one to profess his creed and view of life, be it Christian or heathen.

William Michelsen

1. Universal Historical Learning

Five hundred years have now passed since the time of Dante, from which point we usually date the rebirth of learning. We Norsemen may well be astonished at this, when we realise that Dante was born at the end of the century of Valdemar II, Haakon IV, Saxo, and Snorri Sturluson[1], with which age the Norse spirit expired. But idle astonishment was never more inappropriate than now, when the world is out of joint. If we are to be rescued from the great shipwreck we must learn to wonder only a moment, even at the strangest sight, and then work with twice the energy and with serene composure. Instead of becoming immersed in pointless speculation over the mysterious course of destiny we must strive to understand only as much of it as we need for the moment in order to recognize our calling and proceed on our designated path. For clarity, deep and total, all-penetrating clarity must indeed be the goal for all endeavour with an awareness of life and spirit; but the very fact that it is the goal and the crown makes it impossible for it also to be the staff on our journey, or the helmet that adorns the head in battle. Never therefore has the enemy of the human race hatched so pernicious a lie as the one that clarity should be the birthmark of light and palpability the birthmark of truth. For nothing under the sun tempts the brightest and best souls so much as the appearance of perfection; yet nothing is more certain than that those who clutch at it miss the mark, which they then do not only lose sight of, but turn away from.

It is clearly this disastrous mistake that has not only made many of the deepest thinkers into false guides in the circle they wished to enlighten, but has turned the life of the outstanding nations, both past and present, into great tragedies with the result that an enthusiastic youth and an active manhood gave way only to spiritless, naked old age, where they childishly reach out for chimeras and play with shadows, until they sink into gloom, learning too late that all appearances deceive and that human life perishes through the very enlightment that turns into a shadow.

Thus it must neither surprise nor distress us that the Italian erudition, which was always an illusory idea and produced only shadows in the spiritual world, has in reality passed away with the last century, and like its own shadow strives in vain to rise again in our time. But we must realise that now it is our turn. Either learning must perish, or it must be reborn in Scandinavia on a higher level. I say in the North because it is there that the spirit must have its starting-point, though not its limits. For if we go back to the thirteenth century, when the spiritual development of the Norsemen was cut short unfulfilled, and it would seem, untimely so, then we see that in the previous five or six centuries, say from the year 700, a kindred spiritual endeavour extended throughout England, our Scandinavia and part of Germany, begun by the emigrant Anglo-Saxons and with the Danes and Icelanders ending the period as its chroniclers.

This time, however, it is the aboriginal Norsemen and not the emigrant ones who must be the spirit's main wheel or there will be no Scandinavian learning. For the emigrant kinsmen are either degenerate, or they have lost so much of their old Norse character that it is a question whether they will even join the movement; there is no question of them leading it, that would be quite impossible. Never, therefore, have we Norsemen been addressed by the signs of the times more earnestly than now; never has so clear a call from the spirit of man gone out to us with the great question – Are you willing to give up the crown your fathers and your emigrant kinsmen have fought so bravely for, or will you with serene composure follow in the old footsteps and imitate, not those who make heroic gestures, but those who take heroic strides, which can be imitated only by taking them? If you want the latter, if you want the best, says the spirit, then consider what is lacking in that idea of development of the life of man, which dissolved into emptiness and impotence. Dare to grasp the idea of man in all its mysteriousness, both high and low, heavenly and earthly, if you ever wish to see it illuminated. And fight like Norsemen, with united strength and with the mutual sacrifice of all the individuality that honesty and truthfulness do not sanction, and which is therefore as incompatible with true wisdom as with true love. Do not brood, but seek light where the testimony of the ages shows you it can be found, and walk and work in that light: then you will become its children, discover its secrets and inherit its glory. Do not brood over what cannot possibly be comprehended until it has been experienced, but use your life for what is worthy of it and what can set it in the light. And do not hesitate; for now every second is precious, now the tribes are casting lots in our world for the last time. 'Too late' are the worst words of all, for they mean that everything is forfeited.

It is clear to any spirit friendly or hostile, good or bad, that the learning that was most recently cultivated received its death-blow during the French Revolution and must either perish, like the learning of the Greeks, the Romans and the Norsemen, or be transfigured into a higher one that can revive it. For everywhere it is cut off from the life of people, that is it is dead, and in its present form, like everything that is dead, it is hostile to the life of man. And no wonder that this Italian, or neo-Roman, this monastic-Latin, papist spiritual culture, which from its very beginning was an artefact, like Dante's Divine Comedy, and at best a hothouse plant, cannot prolong its days beyond the five centuries, the age of the Phoenix, that seem to be the numbered days for all cultures, since not even those of Greece and Scandinavia, although they sprang from the life of the people and were thus in sympathy with it, could exceed that period of time? Actually I said it *almost* disappeared with the last century; for it has perished on the continent and is resuscitated in vain, so that it is only in England that it still has a sort of existence, as will be seen when Dante's death, like Frey's in Uppsala[2] can no longer be kept secret there, or when the collossal colleges of Oxford and Cambridge topple down and smash in the process everything that leant on them for support. And these great and glorious monuments, not to petty, dull and lifeless erudition, which has only abused them, but to the spirit of the Anglo-Saxons and the Normans that has been more or less excommunicated from them, they must soon topple unless they are reformed better than the so-called radical reformers wish[3], for their reforms would only totally destroy them.

My pen cannot therefore express how fervently I wish that I had a voice that could be heard, not just on this side of the Sound and the Dovre mountains, but on the other side of the North Sea as well, and an oration on my lips to persuade all those in whom there still runs a drop of Norse blood, reflecting a spiritual life, in order to unite them and lay the foundation of a new Danish spiritual culture and learning, living, popular and all-embracing, while the ruins of the past might still be saved and used to advantage.

However, if my pen cannot even express my wish, being dumb from its mother's womb, even less can it speak for my view of the present, of life and of learning. So when I nevertheless attempt to describe it, it is only in the hope that wherever people will lend an ear to the voice of truth and the advice of wisdom, there will also be eyes to see and tongues to speak freely of the demands of the spirit and the needs of the time.

I assert first that there is no country where the Roman-Italian learning is so firmly established as in England, where quite independent of the state it has sufficient means for its existence so long as the rights of property are upheld, and where the people have had a passion for whatever it hatched, more or less every day, over the centuries: gigantic mechanical contraptions and parliamentary fulminations. So when it topples there, there is nowhere it can be saved.

But I also assert that this learning is not worth saving, for it is hostile to all real life in the world of the spirit and is therefore so far from leading us to an explanation of life and death that, on the contrary, it has been guiding us all its days towards renunciation of the spirit and the spiritual death of the people, except when Luther for a moment harnessed it to the triumphal car of the spirit.

Finally I maintain that when one regards the world of the spirit with Norse eyes in the light of Christianity, one gets the impression of an universal historical development of art and learning that embraces the whole life of man, with all its energies, conditions and achievements. This idea liberates, strengthens and delights all that is in harmony with the temporal welfare of the individual, the nations and the whole race of man, and which must of necessity lead to the most perfect explanation of life that is possible in this world. This Graeco-Norse or new-Danish way of life and culture is what gives the Norse myths, in which it is latent, their universal historical significance, and for us especially an inestimable worth. It is this learning I wanted to portray here, both in its nature and in its contrast to the Romano-Italian life curse and spiritual tedium.

To be sure, I find it embarrassing to have to describe something that, like life in its contrast to death, can only be expressed by a living voice, and also to have to discuss in passing something that demands from us a painstaking argument. But it is my hope that the thoughts of Norse readers need only be directed to the Roman monster, and to the heroic Norse race, which gave this Frost-Giant[4] its death-blow, for them to see far more clearly than I can depict, how terrible it is for humanity and how shameful for the heroic sons of the North that the badly exorcized ghost of the giant has risen from the Pontine marshes and for five hundred years, now deceptively in a friendly guise, now as an open enemy, has oppressed the nations, pecking out their eyes in an eagle's shape and drinking the blood of their hearts.

It is not only by law of nature that a nation's literature must be congenial to the nation – and what an abomination the Roman then must be! – but it is also a historical fact that nearly all of Roman literature, particularly the poetry, is imitation work, and unlike the Greek and Old Norse did not spring from the life of the people and has not been lovingly cultivated over the centuries. On the contrary, it was produced on a basis of sale and return and put out for show, mostly in the days of the tyrant Augustus, to flatter his ears and gild the chains that through Rome's art and wit had been forged for the people around the great Mediterranean Ocean, and which had now become a well-deserved reward, for itself to wear, that is a plain, unshakable truth. And what sort of an art and learning should develop out of such a literature when in addition it had become the corpse of a dead language, – that was easy to predict. But it has been a heavy lot to bear, as heavy as the Roman yoke in all its forms – like the chains in the hands of the Roman Emperor, like the crozier in the hand of the Roman Pope and like the rod in the hand of the Latin schoolmaster. It fell to Norsemen and the Germans to break these chains and it was their joy to snap the crozier, but so far they have respectfully kissed the rod, although it was the most dangerous and pernicious weapon in the murderer's hidden hand; for it scared the life out of the mother and whipped it out of the children so that they never became men enough to break it.

But broken it will be, whatever we do, just as the chains would have been broken by the barbarians if there had been no Goths, and the crozier by the atheists if Luther had never existed. That, however, is not of the spirit; to mankind it cannot be the same whether the rod is broken by the Jacobins or radicals, by the uncivilized mob and the insubordinate schoolboys, or by the educated, sensible champions of art and learning – any more than history would have had a similar passage if the Gauls and not the Anglo-

Saxons had succeeded the Romans in Britain, or Attila rather than Theodoric had become lord of Rome, or if Vanini[5] and not Luther had been the scourge of the Pope.

No, the question is now as always whether, when the hour of the tyrant strikes because his cup of sin is full, he will merely change his name and grow viler as he ages, or he really is to be overthrown and wiped out. It is a question of whether we are to have a neo-Franconian barbarism which will be the equivalent of the old-Franconian after the fall of Rome and the destruction of the Goths, or a new-Danish advance transfiguring the old-Danish that rose up on the ruins of Rome throughout the northern hemisphere. My vote goes to the latter; that is what I have been working for all my days, and I hope to enjoy the sight of it in my evening hour without being terrified by the ambiguous omens I have so far seen. These omens, though by no means delusions, are still for the most part evoked by the twilight I could not possibly avoid as I worked my way out of an Egyptian gloom, but which I have now passed beyond.

So when I now speak of a new-Danish development, I do not take the Word Danish in the restricted sense which I have often used before now and even more often used as a term of praise. I mean it in the old Norse sense, when Danish stretched not just from the Ejder to Tromsø, and from the North Sea to the Gulf of Finland, but also across the ocean to the Norse people on the remote Isle of Hercules[6]. Similarly, when I speak of the rebirth of a Christian and old-Danish learning, I do not mean two things that only a poet can get into rhyme, nor do I mean something specifically Christian bound to the Christian faith. I mean rather a Graeco-Norse development which with the aid of the Mosaic-Christian way of thinking will be a living advance and a universal historical one.

For whether one is a Christian or a heathen (Naturalist), one cannot possibly be a historian with a glimpse of the spirit, without immediately seeing that in fact it was neither the Scythians nor the Barbarians, but the superior Christian way of thinking that in the days of Rome gloriously shattered the chains of humanity. And it was the same way of thinking, reborn in Luther, that laid the Roman Pope on his death-bed. And it is this way of thinking alone that has set its universal human stamp on the mentality on the education, and on the learning of the new world of nations. This stamp was lacking in the ancient world; and even the monster of Rome, though it has abused it, has not managed to obliterate it.

Such a spiritless and lifeless learning as the Romano-Italian, which by its nature knows no other elucidation than dissolution; which takes pride in dissolving all things spiritual into thin air and the godhead into the four elements; and which was drawn by the golden age of Augustus only as wolves are by human corpses and worms are by the plague, such a learning must naturally regard Christianity, which obviously interrupted Roman enlightenment and Roman felicity, as really a great disaster so it is no wonder that it explains the surprising effects of Christianity from sheer enthusiasm and fanaticism, and lies and superstition, which, however, the worldy wise will refer to by more urbane and better-sounding names. But one does not need be either an ape or a Roman because one is a heathen; that has been sufficiently demonstrated by the poetry and history of Greece and ancient Scandinavia in particular. And so long as one remains a real human being and feels oneself to be essentiallly different from the dumb creatures and strangely related to the immortal gods, and spoken to kindly by the spirit of God and Man in all the tongues that are known — well then, one bows in deepest admiration to the spirit that on the Apostles' glowing tongues issued forth in the living word from Jerusalem and worked miracle upon miracle for the good of man to the ends of the earth — the spirit that opens the human eye to see down the wonderful path that awaits the jointly begotten children of heaven and earth, and opens for them a smiling view across the sea of death to the land of the living in the eternal kingdom of the Father of Mankind.

Be he Christian or heathen, Turk or Jew, every man who is aware of his spiritual nature is in himself such a glorious mystery that he casts absolutely nothing aside merely because it is strange and seems as inexplicable as himself. On the contrary, he is almost irresistibly drawn to what is strange — because at heart it resembles himself, and because in it he expects to find the answer to his own mystery — an answer he cannot possibly expect from something he can see through in a trice. Therefore such a person, whether in fact he is of this or that creed has or has no particular faith at all with regard to God, never finds himself attracted by transparently enlightened persons, whose whole wisdom one can learn by heart in an hour and possibly even explain to wise dogs. Rather is he attracted precisely by the mysterious and deep natures that sense more than they see, feel much deeper than they can fathom, and speak with far greater enthusiasm than they themselves are aware of. And there are undoubtedly quite a number of such people here in Scandinavia who, despite all the Roman enlightenment, shun it like the plague rather than they shun poetry; for I myself have met many both as a lecturer and as a writer.

It is for this reason that I am sure that when Scandinavia awakes, and all ancient peoples must awake in our troubled times, then many will lend an ear to the view that, be it now poetical and historical, of natural or supernatural origin, the Mosaic-Christian way of thinking is the only genuine view of human life. By manifesting itself when all the gods of the heathens were extinct, when all spirit had disappeared and eternity was merely an empty notion, through this and through its unequalled and blessed achievements through eighteen centuries it has genuinely guaranteed its own and Christ's divinity; so, it is that way of thinking which in learning as well as in life, must be the lode star we endeavour to follow. Only must we consider before this can happen, not only the difference between Christianity and Bible faith, but also between Christian faith and the Christian way of thinking, and though we seem far from it, the difference is nonetheless both so evident and so important that understanding of this must be near at hand.

It must of necessity be realised by all enlightened people in the serious, historical Scandinavia that the quarrel and the point at issue between Christians and Naturalists is by no means the divinity of Christ and the Christian way of thinking, the divine effects of which through eighteen centuries are an unassailable proof, the quarrel is a quite different one, which may well be correctly expressed in theological terms as the question of Christ's eternal divinity but which historically expresses itself clearly in the contrary belief about natural man. That natural man is created in the image of God and had in the breath of life from God all that he required to reach his great destiny as a son of God, on that point everyone with spirit in them must agree. And that very early on a great accident befell him that brought the earth around him into an oblique inclination to the heavens, time into a disparity with eternity and human nature into a confusion, this is proved so loud and clear by everyday and universal historical experience that no person with a glimmer of spirit and a spark of truthfulness to him can deny it. The main question is not even what we are to call this great accident, for although, of course, the Naturalist does not like the word 'fall', which like all falls sounds a bit flat, and would rather say error or aberration, yet since both terms may be used and since it is undeniable that every deviation from the natural course must for a spiritual creature be regarded as sin and lead to a fall, the Naturalist must realize it is not worth quarrelling over that either. The point at issue is only whether the injury can be healed by natural means or not. And that is our great church quarrel in which all mediation must be regarded as ridiculous; for here there is no middle way but an infirmity of purpose that must either be the transition to a particular faith or paralyse all activity and send us crashing into the bottomless pit of self-contradiction, which is everlasting death and the spirit's hell. On the other hand when we become totally aware of our division, and endeavour, each in his particular church to articulate them, we shall no longer fear to be in agreement about everything that can be true under both assumptions. Not until then can experience show whether it is the Christians or the Naturalists who went astray, for by its fruits shall the tree be known. But as long as we continue to be bundled together in one church, all that we do is chaotic, and a quarrel, as bitter as it is pointless, is unavoidable. For the Christians believe that through the Fall human nature has become so corrupted that all true healing is impossible, but they celebrate Baptism as a true rebirth in water, in which the believer is spiritually recreated. To raise this new person to a divine union with the Saviour and the Divine Man, Jesus Christ, is the task of their church, both individually and in general. The Naturalist cannot possibly admit this without being guilty of a monstrous contradiction, but must declare this faith to be a great misunderstanding, which, though unable to annihilate the divine effects of the Christian way of thinking, has nonetheless weakened it greatly and prevented enlightenment. So on the contrary he has to claim that the old human nature both can and must be healed, so that it is in no way the purpose of Christianity to be absorbed into Christ, but only that one must spiritually absorb Him into oneself, as the divine example of what we must all be cleansed and clarified for: children of man who raise themselves to God's children. People with spirit will immediately perceive how all important this genuine discrepancy is, without it making any more difference to the history of our Christian way of thinking than the contrary theories in astronomy do to our contemplation of the heavens. In fact it makes the same difference, inasmuch as we derive the same phenomena from contrary grounds, for in both cases it is only a question of whether the sun goes round the earth or the earth round the sun, so that it is only fools who delude themselves that the earth has its own light or that day follows night without either the earth turning towards the sun anew, or the sun the earth, which means, spiritually speaking, either God's son becomes the Son of Man or the Son of Man becomes God's son.

Not until we realise this, so that we face one another as Chaldeans and Copernicans in the spiritual world, not disagreeing so much about the world itself as about its laws, not until then can we set up schools together without either fighting about the books or, as they do in Peder Paars, fighting with them. But we can do that too; and we can realize on both sides that insofar as books can decide our quarrel it must be those books that have been explained in depth. However, the matter can in fact only be decided by the illumination of human life that books cannot express, but can only describe, and it is therefore no use whatever our pulling books by the hair since that will not change life, but merely abuse it.

We go then to books not as bookworms who will feed on them as we would feed on corpses and carcasses, but as living people who wish to learn from books what we cannot tell ourselves – namely, how human life manifested itself in days gone by, what obstacles it met, how it overcame them, and what we can deduce from this about the nature and character of human life as well as the best way of developing it and making use of it.

Thus, if we consider all books as being contributions to the history of human life – in the whole human family, in the different races and in the individual – we can see emerging a quite different scholarship from the deadly pedantry we have to renounce in our schools as the work of frost-giants; a scholarship that not only extends to all that is knowable, but embraces it as a living idea and with a common purpose, which is the elucidation of human life in all its directions and relationships. Then scholarship becomes truth in practice – when it invariably starts from life and aims at an elucidation of it. For then we value everything according to its relationship to and its influence on life, generally and specifically, and the most beneficial consequences cannot fail to follow; no nation amongst whom such a scholarship is zealously pursued can be blind to its importance.

But what is this common scholarship to consist of; what must every student learn?

When we study for the sake of life, it goes without saying that we need to know in particular the powerful manifestations of life that no longer occur in everyday experience. For it is ridiculous to wish to learn from books something that repeats itself daily before our very eyes, and something that we can find far more easily amongst ourselves. And it is above all the misty ancient times that we all need to study. For those days were the young days of the race, obviously days of spirit and imagination, the prophetic age, when forces were prominent which are now only inactive and weak. And it is really ridiculous to organize and evaluate forces according to their weakest after-effects; so if we want to understand the old age of mankind we must first know about its youth.*

There cannot be any disagreement about this amongst men of spirit, and since we have books from really only three of the ancient peoples who are all major peoples in universal history, that is, the Hebrews, the Greeks and the Romans, there can be no question of their books not continuing to be the main books in the grammar school. So it is only a matter of appreciating and using them quite differently. In other words the languages must be learned for the sake of the books, and the books read for the sake of life, instead of, as has hitherto been the case, more or less using life to read the books and reading them for the sake of the language. This perverse Black Book[8] reading-method, whereby we read the spirit out of ourselves as if it was the devil himself, must simply be banned, if life is not to perish but to be illuminated in our schools.

Now, to want to cobble together from a few books a mumbo-jumbo of one's own that was no use for anything, except for making pompous perorations at a lectern, is such a deadly idea that even if it had not been the Roman monster's ghost one thereby strove to conjure up, and even if it had not resulted in the fearful composition slavery that beats the life out of young people the way repeated sowing of oats exhausts the soil, still the spirit on its first arrival at school would have had to drop all thought of such waste

---

* If one considers the ancient books as documents of the spiritual history of the race and the corresponding nations, one always begins quite naturally with political history, since it is the events of the visible world that provide a firm basis for one's view and create an interest in the nation.

of time and soul-destruction, we must of necessity learn the language of the Roman brigand; not only was his career so remarkable but also his language is the key to so great a deal of Medieval literature and to the Romance languages that none of us can do without it. But to torture the life out of young people, that is a task for slaves, not for free-born Danes, nay divine Asir and Vanir.

But should the educated then not have their own language to be used among themselves? By no means! They must not have a language of their own making, which is of no use whatsoever and is pernicious in every way, since nothing is more inimical to human life and the mother tongue of the people than a language composed of dead letters and then idolized as a model language. The sad experience of five hundred years has made this so dreadfully clear that the spirit that is wakening is tempted rather to do something it must on no account allow itself – that is, banish all dead languages from the ordinary school.

But the educated must not merely be allowed to use a language that will give them an excellent acquaintance with ancient times, they must rather be made to use it. For it will only have the most beneficial consequences so long as it remains a real and a living language and young people are not tortured by it but rather guided and encouraged towards it. Nor can there be any doubt about this choice; for only one of the three major classical languages, Greek, is still a living language; and since it also gives access to the only ancient literature that can truly be called by that name, then everyone with spirit can only agree about this.

Very likely the school for death will once again propose a middle course; that is, make Classical Greek the language of scholars. For if one could get away with stepping from one grave to another, then death would still be vindicated. But the spirit will not be mocked, and therefore Modern Greek it must and shall be, first and last for the sake of life, that great advantage that nothing can compare with, much less be a match for, but also because experience teaches us that children learn to read and write best when they have first learned to speak, even if the language of books is as different from what they hear at home as the Danish in our books is different from the speech of the Jutlanders. And Ancient Greek is no farther from Modern Greek than that.

This step out of the grave to living people is the giant stride which scholarship must make in order to become a national blessing instead of a national scourge. For as soon as the living language which brings acquaintance with the spirit of Homer, Hercules and Plato, becomes the language of educated people, then the whole world of scholarship will inevitably receive life, and receive through it both the conditions and the reason for living industry and progress. At that point the competitive spirit and even ambition itself will be beneficial to life and learning; in brief, the school will of its own accord get into its true historical and Nordic shape. Then scholars will use their language, in a different way from Latin, for the good it can promote: to penetrate deeper into the spirit of antiquity and to facilitate the exchange of ideas amongst scholars.* But naturally not to disfigure the mother tongue or force it out of the class-room, which is precisely the place where it must be heard in all its power and fullness. Yes, indeed, when we break free of Rome, where they had slaves as schoolmasters, and come to Greece, where it was the highest honour for the most outstanding brains, the noblest and most eloquent men to be listened to by those eager for knowledge, and even by light-hearted youngsters, then the days of slavery for schoolmasters and schoolchildren are over and every stage in the grammar school will see a lively and instructive entertainment in which fatheads soon learn the best thing they can from their school: that is, to pack their bags and go, because it will never occur to anyone, for their sake either to make life a misery for himself or to spoil the Olympic game for those who both can and will compete for the prize.

Now that was the scholarly relationship to the history of the human race in antiquity. But the scholars of the North cannot and must never forget that the North also has a heroic age of its own to which they have a double relationship, both a closer one and a deeper one. For Norsemen are the fourth major people in universal history, a fact that needs to be known before one can understand the life and history of the Middle Ages and modern times. And the

* Latin, being composed of letters, was already in the books more a point at issue than a bond between scholars, and since the English especially wished to be masters in their own house, there grew up and there still exist two widely differing systems of pronouncing Latin: the English and the Italian. The result is that, just like at Babel, one Latinist does not understand the other. Whereas, if we learn Modern Greek, we will naturally strive to speak like the Greeks, and to read like them, and then the tie is both real and living.

living key to Old Norse literature is the Icelandic language, so that needs to be learnt both for the sake of the ancient books and for the new literary language which will always need to borrow from it and be illuminated by it. What is required for this, however, is so little and so easy for us in Denmark that it will be a game, not a burden, at school. And in Scandinavia, furthermore, it will link the culture of the learned with that of the people in the most natural and best possible way.

Indeed, popular knowledge or folk culture and education in the proper spiritual sense, is the second giant stride that simply must be made immediately whereever disintegration is to be revented, folk-life to be saved and scholarship to prosper

The necessity of this has long been felt, for it was precisely the feeling of the unnatural and the deadly in the ruling Latin scholarship, hostile to everything practical and living, that led to enthusiasm for Rousseau's and Basedow's vagaries in the previous century and which has produced all ferment in educational thought. It has not yet led to any satisfactory result, but it must do so, or it will lead to barbarism. The attempt to popularize the Grammar School and the University during this ferment was natural, but only because they wished, although without spirit, to transform the world of the spirit, which of course cannot be done. That this would lead to barbarism was soon apparent; but it was not clear that it would just as surely and far more violently lead to a perpetration of the odious Latin malpractice with still more earnestness and strictness than before. And this must be realized if either the people or scholarship is to be saved, and with God's help both of them *shall* be saved.

We must realize that scholarship is one thing and education and fitness for life, as a person and as a citizen, another; both things may well be united, but not amongst the general crowd, and they must in no way be hostile to one another but must be kept apart, since otherwise they each tend to crowd the other out and unavoidably disfigure and corrupt one another.

For education and fitness for life must always be suited to the folk-life of the present, whereas scholarship is for human life in general. So when scholarship is really genuine, it includes education and fitness for life, but these cannot include it except as a vague feeling that scholarship, particularly amongst the scholars proper (the schoolmasters), will lead us astray if there is no education of the people at hand forcing it to take the present life and the present moment into account, just as the folk-culture will deteriorate into a superficial gloss unless scholarship keeps it alive.

If one is truly wise, one will always want to become wiser, and thus learn from enemies as well as from friends. The latest prevailing self-conceit that made wind with the philosopher's stone and claimed that whoever wished to be wiser than Tom, Dick and Harry was either already mad or well on the way to being so, was, as we can see, simply crass stupidity. Thus all wise school systems must be based on progressive enlightenment and education. So that if we are so vain as to turn our children and the whole of posterity into a life-size lithograph of ourselves, we are both a disgrace to ourselves and we are also doing our best to make all future generations unhappy, because Man is not an ape, destined first to ape the other animals and then himself until the world's end. Rather is he a glorious incomparable creature, in whom divine powers shall proclaim, develop and enlighten themselves through thousands of generations as a divine experiment to show how spirit and dust can permeate one another and be transfigured into a common divine consciousness. That is how Man must be regarded if there is to be a spiritual scholarship on earth; and that is how Man is regarded wherever the Mosaic-Christian way of thinking was an inspiration. And the history of this view proves that it is neither an empty figment of the imagination nor something foreign to Man, but that the more one made it one's own, life adapted itself to it in a natural if also miraculous, glorious and blessed way. In the world of scholarship, however, this view has never come to dominate, because the ancient spirit, just as its Italian ghost was lifeless, was based on writing the dead letter instead of on the living word. It therefore relentlessly promoted not life but death, leading Man to the grave instead of to heaven; in fact it led him down through the range of the animal kingdom back to the worms, instead of up the heavenly ladder to the Creator. In England and in Iceland the ancient Norse scholarship made a weak attempt to attach itself to heaven and to the life of the people; but its powers were divided and the Norseman's age of scholarship had not yet arrived. Thus the attempt may well have been beneficial, have delayed death and have had incalculable, unknown consequences, but in general it was a failure. Now, however, it is only a matter of will-power, for now the time and the inclination are there for all to see, now all our resources are held in readiness and the great book of experience is opened, the book that can teach us how to avoid all the rocks and whirlpools that have hitherto brought death and destruction with them, and how to weather the storms that cannot be avoided on the great ocean. To try to make everybody equally wise at once is folly. If it is seriously attempted, it will only serve to make everybody equally stupid. But to offer practically the same education to all classes and to open to all the path to continuous progress is, like everything that leads to the free but methodical development of one's powers, not only wise, but absolutely necessary now, if nations and states are to prosper.

A gentlemen's academy or whatever we call such a higher institution for education in national culture and practical proficiency in all the major subjects, is obviously an urgent need in every country which must be met as soon as possible for the sake of society and for the sake of learning.

With my knowledge of history I neither am nor can be any friend of parliaments; but since they are the order of the day, it must be realized that unless a suitable education is provided for all those who may become members of the popular assembly, they will be a disaster for the state in general and for learning in particular. One needs to treasure it before one willingly contributes to its treasury.

Such an institution must have sprung from learning and must maintain a living relationship with it, if it is not to become harmful or to stagnate. On the other hand it must be independent so as not to become just a tail or an empty shadow, since it must be a true, spiritual power through which life and the present day assert their inalienable rights which are so easily disregarded by scholars. For here the land of our fathers with all its natural and historical character will be related to real life and the demands of the present day. There will be the common centre from which the institution branches out into all the main lines of practical life, and back to which it endeavours to gather and unite all the energies of society. Here, all the civil servants of the state who need not scholarship but life, insight and practical ability, and all those who wish to belong to the rank of the educated should get the very best chance of developing themselves in a suitable direction and of getting to know one another. Here the national literature will also serve the purpose and receive the encouragement without which it is only an ornamental flower, soon to wither and die; and while education

50

was being made fruitful among the people the life of the people would enrich scholarship.*

Naturally at such an institution in Scandinavia there must be an opportunity to learn Icelandic, without anyone being forced to do so. This is not just because it is a natural and fine way for academic and popular education to meet, but especially because a number of the State's non-academic civil servants need it, and all educated readers amongst us would benefit from it.

This, however, does not represent a living bond between academic and popular education, but where the state has a clergy, they of necessity will be the living and invaluable bond. For according to the Christian way of thinking the delightful historical fact about the clergy is that it must endeavour to be both scholarly and popular. It cannot of course be both at the highest level, but insofar as learning is revived and the people educated, it will become a real and a living bond between both; both scholar and layman must recognize this as being a great earthly blessing, however they may regard the state clergy's guidance towards eternity.

A fine ideal, one might say; just too bad that it cannot be put into practice in the real world.

But why not? If it has been possible to introduce and maintain in the real world scholarship and learning which are derived from such a false idea and empty speculation as they obviously are: with death to beautify life, and with books, especially in Latin, to improve the mother tongue and patch up its deficiencies, then it must also be possible to apply an idea to real life, which has its source there, and which is invested with the power to protect, develop, enlighten and illuminate it in every possible direction, excluding from itself only Death's dominion, which can in no way be compatible with

---

* It is obvious that together with many others all teachers in the secondary schools and the village schools will receive their training here and then become the main organs of the national spirit. But with our Romano-Germanic prejudices, we shall doubtless find it hard to realize that the education of lawyers for the civil service also ought to be transferred from the university to the citizens' college, although both legal history and the nature of the things make it plain enough. One ought to study our laws at the university as an important part of political history and as a historical attempt to adapt the law to interests of the state and the character of the people. But the idea that the civil servants lawyers must be either bookworms or philosophers of law is perverse and most harmful.

life, but creates only corpses and shadows in the real world and there are enough of them already without one working day and night to get more. Besides, Death has now been ruling for so long that according to my view of history, do we have nowhere the alternative means of saving ourselves, and where there is only one way, whether one believes it will help or not, one cannot possibly be wrong to choose it, and the sooner the better. For I cannot but think that the revolutions, like death agonies, must run their course through the new world of nations and dissolve the learned and the lay society in the process unless they are prevented from doing so by a reform of the school-graveyard into a seed-school for life so that it is given both the permission to develop and the light to see what truly serves its temporal peace and comfort. I use the word "temporal" deliberately; for although within the church I advise everybody to forget as far as possible the temporal in favour of the eternal, and although I am sure that whoever follows this advice properly will not regret it in this life and even less in eternity; nevertheless with the state and the school it is quite another matter. For neither of them can last for ever, so they cannot possibly give us the eternal life they themselves do not have, and must therefore only aim at living as long and at giving as much temporal benefit as possible. This is particularly necessary in our time, since nearly all of us care only very little about eternity, or we think that we ourselves can best provide for it. So that if we do not believe that the state and the school benefit us in the temporal life, it is at most a matter of indifference to us what happens to them. Then society and its institutions are quite clearly on shifting soil, if everyone who is not paid to maintain them is at least indifferent to their fate. Here is the key to the events of both yesterday and tomorrow, and at least in England and the North it will be thanks to the schoool if the towers topple. For in England the school is free, and in Scandinavia the governments have shown that at least they would like to arrange it so that both learning and popular education could be promoted to the benefit of real life, if the academics could just tell them how it could best be done. So the trouble is only that a learning that comes from death and leads to death cannot possibly be compatible with the life of the people, and a popular education that is derived from the dead, spiritless concept of Man and all things human cannot possibly safeguard either the state or the school but can only topple both, since it is incompatible with the inhuman animal selfishness and self-conceit that are assiduously developed in us all from the cradle. Thus wherever the noble-minded and the wise fail to gain the insight that we were blind tools of Rome's spirit-lessness or of a false idea that must not merely be relinquished but combated by the true one, if it is not to destroy everything that we appreciate in this world – where they cannot do that, human fortune is lost. But where there is a true desire both to live and to be educated as a Man, as is the case wherever the spirit of Scandinavia is natural, there the truth of experience cannot help but triumph, once it makes itself heard.

'Makes itself heard'. I use the words deliberately, and not just as words printed in a book. For every truth that is written but not spoken can never be written with sufficient diligence and art in the book of *forgetfulness* to make it living and active. Therefore, the few who, in spite of the "black death", have miraculously become aware of life and gained the courage to spit the ink out of their mouths, must make themselves heard wherever the school seriously desires the well-being of the state and of mankind. For even if one believes it cannot do any good, nonetheless it ought to be tried, since it is quite clearly in our time that it must either endure of perish.

That being so, I for my part am sure that it will endure in Scandinavia, and that it would endure in England too if with their hawk's eye for everyday experience they were not blind to the universal-historical, or if, with every possible freedom to open their mouths, they nevertheless regrettably did not have a mouth under a pair of eyes that see where the error lies. For there is no lack of an ear over there, and through a good ear the eyes of the spirit may be opened; whereas sticking people in the eyes, even with the best steel nibs, only makes people furious at the fingers which seem to be looking for a good excuse to put their eyes out.[10]

So assuming that a genuine desire arises in the North to live and see good days in the world of the spirit, only then will the old books prove useful and then we shall get new ones not just for our wonderment, but also for our delight.

Dear reader, do not think we have got more than enough books, but consider that there is precisely the same difference between books as there is between writers and readers, so that we have both too many and too few. And it is only in the case of the bad ones that the lesser is the better. When therefore the spirit becomes both the author and the critic, both the censor and the librarian, then our reader may be confident that the collection of books will both decrease and improve to our hearts' content.

It is certainly a fearful sight for every scholar of spirit to observe the enormous heaps of books which in particular German scribblers have piled up in the course of the last three centuries. But what the river of time has done of its own accord to the books of antiquity, it will also do to those of more recent date, if it is diverted into our Augean stables with a little Herculean wit. Thus what flowed out of the Styx will fall into the Lethe. For if we can get to know antiquity from the couple of full shelves we have, then we can certainly get to know the age which lies closest to us without reading ourselves to death on book fair catalogues and what they have to offer. Admittedly, we need more books from the Middle Ages than from antiquity, since feeling will ramify more than imagination and the greatest number of all from the Age of Reason, when there are as many minds as there are heads. But all things in moderation. One fathead and one blockhead may be enough for our children to exercise their wit on when they are still in smock-frocks and even from mediocre brains one book can be enough as long as it is in the right place. So in fact it is only the top brains that are worth collecting and anatomizing for the good of all. For if you know the schoolmaster very well, you do not ask him about the knowledge of all the schoolboys, for then you have bought the grocer and got the groceries into the bargain. And that is how it is whichever way you turn. For in history you skip over all the copies together with all the quarrels about the Emperor's beard and all the wise accounts of what Bloggins would have thought and how he would have acted if he had been in the great men's shoes, and we all know why he was not. And finally, in poetry we are well aware that it is only the major poets who create their own world, which the others get lightfingered about. And since the art of stealing and concealing is daily on the increase, they content themselves in the History of Literature with hanging the biggest thieves and letting the small ones escape – or rather letting them paddle their own canoe until they capsize and drown.

But if we have too many books from the early days of printing, just as we have too many sharpshooters from the age of gunpowder, then, on the other hand, the books from the Middle Ages are suffering roughly the same fate as its castles, that is, they lie in ruins and may well seem dark as long as they are only illuminated by empty lanterns. But of course they need to be lit up before we can understand them, and they certainly will be when the books come to light – the sort of books that are now being sat on in Rome and Vienna, and mainly in London and Paris. Even Latin books were only grudgingly made available, since they were only written in dog Latin, that is, there were still signs of life in them. And as for what was written in the vernacular, which by comparison was so little that it is priceless, the classical gentlemen found barely a single curiosity worthy of attention, and that they translated for the common good – into Latin lest it spoil taste. Now this is utterly wrong; and especially the old Norse literature in Anglo-Saxon and Icelandic must be published, every scrap of it. For we have to see all the things that those tough warriors who crushed Rome and created a new world of nations were aiming at in every field, and they most certainly were not trifles, even if their achievements in certain areas were not so great.* But on this point good counsel is hard to find. For it will cost a lot of money, and no one can give more than he has got, so it is the Englishman who will have to fork out. And so he will, as soon as he is on the scent and realizes that not only does he himself, as the heir of the Anglo-Saxons own the greatest plot and that here we are talking about nothing less than a Bifrost-Bridge[11] linking two spheres of the world, and an underground tunnel under the currents of time, like Saga's castle with its roof of wawes.[12] For then he will start a 'British and Foreign Printing Society' and that takes care of the rest. To be sure, a great deal of the medieval writings, especially the Latin and the French, will be discarded as soon as they have been read. But they must first be published, since, as you know, a good censor needs Argus eyes, and he will not get them until the book has been printed and fallen into the hands of at least fifty good readers.

Well, so much for the books we do have. As for the books we are going to get, that of course will fall more or less to the lot of posterity to discuss. But I will predict this much, that when the

---

* To the credit of poor little Denmark and to the shame of great, rich England a great deal has been done for Icelandic literature and practically nothing at all for the Anglo-Saxon. However, it must be added that much of the Icelandic still remains unpublished, and that without the rudiments of Icelandic not much can be done for Anglo-Saxon.

Spirit comes to guide the pen of the philologist and the philosopher as well as it does that of the poet, then the reading public will never be offered a book to understand which requires Latin or any other language than the mother tongue, apart from at the most, a bit of Icelandic; nor will laymen or scholars ever be offered comparisons of and investigations into what only a few know or no one knows. But one always begins by giving one's public an accurate and clear survey of the number of facts which lie at the centre of one particular circle of investigation. Only then does one demand that attention be paid to one's conjectures on and one's explanations of these facts, and if they deserve it, they will not fail to get it.

For that matter we can see that just as the enlightenment of human life in all its natural and historical aspects is the lofty goal that ennobles scholarship and unites every informed effort, from the mathematician's to the poet's and from the word-gatherers to the thought-collector's, so will a Universal History, in so comprehensive a sense that the most complete Encyclopedia is its index, be the great work of art that hovers before our sight. And although this great Aladdin's palace cannot possibly acquire its final window here on earth, nevertheless, when all is prepared it will be built in one night by willing and eager spirits. As a wise building-master the human spirit in its most divine alliance made the Bible the foundation of the main building. And for both the wings, which must reflect man's relationship to Nature and History, the foundations were laid by the spirits of Greece and Scandinavia – with a child's hand but in such a way that none after them was capable of continuing the work. For just as we cannot offer chronicles of the world that from a spiritual point of view can surpass Herodotus's Greek History and Snorri's Norse one, so in our letters we have been unable to continue either Greek or Norse literature, which anyway was impossible as long as we at most imitated the one and rejected the other. In both cases this was obviously only the result of our spiritual vacuum and our Roman idolatry. Because it is only when one idolizes the relics of the great thief that one considers it the greatest honour to compete with him in copying the Greeks, and one finds one's superstition being strenghtened every time one sees that it is impossible with his dead fingers to surpass what the living fingers have made. However, as soon as the heroic spirit of the North awakes among us we shall disdain to be slaves of the Romans, and shall not long compete with the Greeks, before we have overtaken them – except, that is, with regard to their mistakes, which we can sedulously avoid. Through the language of the Greeks we acquire their spirit, but only in order to be served by it, not enslaved. For the lustre, as the mark of perfection, when too early achieved is a beautiful mistake, from which one can, of course, learn a great deal but by which one is far easier dazzled, so a little barbarity must persist in a nation that has not the heart to forsake, in return for at beautiful surface, the least bit of the depth and the substance, which in both art and scholarship are the essential thing and must never be sacrificed.

It is at any rate typical of the Romanized nations, or the Romance heroines, the famous mourners of Rome's Adonis, that they never brought Rome beyond embalming his remains (quae supersunt) in Spanish-Egyptian, making-up the mummy in French-Arabic, and enshrining it in a coffin of Italian, or, if you like, Parian-Carrara marble. But the fact that Asa-Thor himself in The British Isles has made it a matter of honour to cut a superb glass lid for the changeling's coffin[13] and has wasted untold energies on half-finishing an underground Herculaneum for Hrungner the Giant's chapel is a blemish in literary history that recalls Shakespeare's words about the ocean not being big enough to wash it clean.* For even if Bacon's people as I hope, now at long last put their hand to this History of Universal Literature, which he so warmly recommends to them[14], nevertheless precious time has been lost, the best efforts have been wasted in the service of the troll, and the angle of vision almost distorted beyond repair.

However, such things need to be said aloud at Oxford and Cambridge, for written fulminations are not the thunder of Thor, but only the fulmen brutum of the Latinists, a fact that we are bewitched enough by the black school to forget all the time and settle for a Roman 'Dixi', where we never said a word but only set down in black and white that we both could and would thunder and lighten; which is less than a half-truth, we do not actually do so.

So instead of ploughing with the Romans' calves and deceiving ourselves into thinking that it makes furrows like Gefion's plough in the Sound[15], even though it apparently does only what my steel

---

* Oh! she is fallen into a pit of ink that the wide sea has drops too few to wash her clean again. Much Ado Act. IV sc. 1.

nib is doing here – making a mark on the paper; and instead of deceiving ourselves with Roman superstition into believing that the pen scolds as it scratches and weeps when it drips, let us see what it can do by pointing at Hercules and Cerberus where they stand as large as life next to one another, like William Shakespeare and Ben Jonson, teaching us at one and the same time both what it is that the Roman spirit has tortured to death and what the spirit of Scandinavia is capable of when it breaks the Roman chains. It is indeed a universal historical fact that the only thing in the literature of the past five centuries that deserves to be compared with the masterpieces of the Greeks is the work of Shakespeare as a creator, or at least as father. And how was he made, this Shakespeare, this new Hercules, not Wieland's (be it his Shakespeare or his Hercules)[16] "man of medium size", but the true hero descended from the gods, who walked through Hell unburnt and as a superfluous proof brought back Cerberus on the leash? Was it perhaps by copying Seneca or rather Aeschylus and his brothers, or perhaps by diligent study of the Stagirite's Poetics and The Tiburite's Ars Poetica as well as the learned commentators Gradus ad Parnassum? Far from it, that would be as remote a possibility as the monkey, when performing its master-turn, outshining us, or as heroes being conceived by a mother who merely hears a story of the feats of others. He knew only small Latin and less Greek, says Cerberus, who in vain tried to look after Shakespeare's classical education, with no luck, says John Bull still, almost with a sigh for that daredevil, that "William the Conqueror" in the world of the spirit.*

So what turned him into the Bragi[17] of modern times was plainly the heroic spirit of the North, which urged him to leave school in time before it was whipped out of him who betokened the Norse-Greek rebellion against the Roman-Turks. Admittedly, only traces

---

* If you know how the English still generally regard Shakespeare, read Ben Jonson's epitaph to him. For they are proud that 'he was not of an age, but for all time,' but they are galled by his 'small Latin and less Greek". And it still costs sweat and a headache every day to bang it into one's brain that 'the star of poets, the sweet swan of Avon was made as well as born'; and that every time a little Athene came hopping out of his brain, she was placed on the anvil to be given her proper shape and a cold heart, I imagine: 'Who casts to write a living line must sweat, (such as thine are) and strike the second heat upon the Muses' anvil'. (From Ben Jonson 'To the Memory of My Beloved Mr William Shakespeare).

of this are still to be seen, but I am sure that posterity will reap the blessed fruits of it.

I am not saying in any way that Shakespeare stands alone in England; no, Spenser and Bacon stand by his side, and in the whole of modern English literature, just as in the language a boxing-match is being fought between Asa-Thor and, Hrungnir, the Giant, offering a much greater and more instructive drama than the German cock-fighting. So I can recommend it as simply the best after the ancient Greek and the old Norse – with the assurance that much more is gained than lost if, to avoid drudgery, one simply skips the rest. I singled out Shakespeare here as the major figure only so that the reader could see from his example that it is just as little a classical education that has raised up English literature as it is the flood of Latin words that adorn and strenghthen the English language, but that, on the contrary, it is in both places the true Norse source of energy that with varying success endeavours to break down the Roman Wall.

And now I will take the opportunity to conclude this preliminary reflection that threatened to go on for ever; since how better can it be concluded than with the best omen for the fall of Rome and the resurrection of the North, that is, with the great prophet of universal historical learning. For that is what William Shakespeare is, and that is why, like all prophets he is honoured most after his death and outside his homeland. Yes, indeed, those of us here who possess the ancient mythical prophecy, we must look with the greatest wonder at how the life of mankind in all its wonderful historical development presented itself to the bard, and how it was struck by the lightning of his prophetic insight, so there will hardly be a single chapter in the great universal history we are awaiting, for which the most suitable heading could not be found in "Shakespeare's Histories", as they are so appropriately called. The fact that he himself never reached any sort of universal historical way of thinking is surely a result of his ignorance of the Norse myths, which merely haunted him, like Hamlet's spirit, and accused their murderer but could find no avenger. But even if he had had both the myths and the vision, he would hardly have produced a corresponding scholarship. For to do so he would really have had to win over Ben Jonson, whom he in fact merely astonished, and who seems to have prized him dearly only after he was dead and could no longer make Falstaff laugh fit to burst at the anvil's eulogy of the sledgehammer. The spirit never wastes its powers, even though it may seem to, and Shakespeare therefore had only what was needed to reawaken the not quite dead battle in the British Isles and in his time to encourage his kinsmen in Germany and in Scandinavia, where the myths were hidden like the heroes of old, until for a second time Rome had sunk into iniquity and its fall was imminent.

Furthermore, the fact that in our time the Hellenes, brutally punished and deeply afflicted under the Roman yoke and the Turkish lash, have risen in rebellion and reawakened the memory of the Lapitha's ancient battle against the Centaurs, and that by doing so they have forced Europe to pay them the attention that classical scholarship was far too Roman to pay, and that is was the Norse seamen who at Navarin were the decisive factor in their liberation, this is the second great and good omen for a Norse-Greek epoch in societies, in art and scholarship, which will surely not fail wherever in Scandinavia or perhaps outside in the British Isles one first hears that the spirit began to speak, and like a lion tore the school sceptre from the claws of the Eagle. It does not really matter to us where the beginning is of what is to our benefit and what brings a glorious epic ending to the great tragedy. But nonetheless the proverb is true that everyone is closest to himself; and if it sounds like a wonderful myth from the Middle Ages that the Danes took refuge so far to the North, because they had sworn rather to bury themselves in the waves than bend themselves beneath the Roman yoke, then we may also hope that it will be recorded for posterity that the Danes shook off the yoke as soon as they were being tricked into wearing it.

Notes

1. Valdemar II (1170-1241), commonly known as "the Victorious", for a short periode held sway over a small Danish empire around the Baltic".
   Haakon V (1204-1263), King of Norway, brought peace and stability to the kingdom after a prolonged period of internal strife about the succession.
   Saxo (1150-1220), called Grammaticus, is the famous author of *Gesta Danorum*, a history of Denmark in Latin, which Grundtvig translated into Danish 1818-1822.
   Snorri Sturluson (1178-1241) is an Icelandic historian and poet

whose *Heimskringla,* a history of the Norvegian kings, is the greatest work of Old Norse literature.

2. Frey or Yngvi-Frey is a mythical king at Uppsala whose death according to Snorri was kept a secret for three years by his warriors.
3. Radical reformers. From his stay in England G. knew of the proposals for reform of the old universities, rejected in 1834.
4. Frost-Giant in Old Norse hrím-thurss. The frost-giants according to Norse mythology were the forces of darkness, cold and barrenness which perished, except for one, when the gods killed the primordial giant Ymir from whose body the world was made. The survivor became the progenitor of the race of gians proper.
5. Lucio Vanini (1585-1819). Italian philosopher who was burned at the stake at Toulouse for atheism and sorcery.
6. Island of Hercules refers to the legend that the first discoverer of Iceland observed at giant on the shore.
7. Grundtvig refers to an episode in Canto III of Ludvig Holberg's mock-heroic poem Peder Paars (1719-20) in which scholars at the University engage in a veritable battle of books.
8. Cyprianus is the name given to a legendary "black book" or grimoire in red print which Scandinavian peasants believed had the power to drive out evil spirits and even to get power over the Devil.
9. Asir and Vanir are the two families of Gods from whom the Danes descended according to Saxo.
10. Grundtvig refers to Isaiah 35, 1-6, but also to the practice of itinerant quacks who at fairs would perform an operation on the eyes of cataract patients that only offered passing relief.
11. Bifrost is the rainbow, "the swaying bridge" which guarded by the god Heimdall links the world of the gods with the human world.
12. Sága is a Norse goddess mentioned in the Edda lay of Grimnismal whose name Grundtvig dexterously confounds with the word *saga,* history, to make her a personification of historiy. The reference to her dwelling-place as roofed by waves is derived from a probably false interpretation of its name, *Søkkvabekkr.*
13. Hrungnir is a giant whom Thor killed in a duel. Hrungnir Grundtvig identifies with Roman culture, the glass lid of his coffin is English classical learning, in particular Gibbon's "Decline and Fall".
14. Baco. G. refers to Francis Bacon's account of history in "the Advancement of Learning" (1623).
15. Grundtvig refers to the myth of Gefion, a goddess, who according so Snorris' Ynglingasaga turned her four sons, fathered by a giant, into calves and harnessed them to a plough with which she carved out a piece of Sweden and dragged into the sea to make the island of Zealand. Grundtvig makes a pun of calf and vellum as well as

of the Danish name for the sound between Sweden and Zealand, "Øresund", which literally may read as "ear-sound".

16. Christopher Martin Wieland (1733-1813) is a German poet who made a prose translation of Shakespeare, which was severely criticised by the Romantics. Among his plays are Hercules's Choice (1773).

17. Bragi is the Norse god of poetry.

IV

The School for Life

The School for Life is part I of Grundtvig's main essay on education "The School for Life and the Academy at Soer", which appeared in 1838. Like Grundtvig's other reflections on education this short essay is a contribution to the debate of the age – partly on the education of children and young people, partly on adult education as the necessary prerequisite for the common man's participation in politics. Since 1660 Denmark had been without a parliament, the King was an absolute ruler. But in 1834 King Frederik VI introduced "advisory assemblies" of "the estates", one for Jutland at Viborg, one for the Danish Isles at Roskilde, and one for Schleswig-Holstein at Rendsburg. In his essay "The Danish Quatrefoil" (1836) Grundtvig described this institution as the "second giant stride" by which "Denmark regained her natural constitution" from the Middle Ages. Here Grundtvig recalls that at the first meeting of these assemblies "a strong plea was made to the King for a School for Life". It was proposed to set up a practical secondary school with instruction in mathematics, natural science, and modern languages beside the disciplines of the grammar school at the old Sorø Academy in Zealand. To Grundtvig's mind that was not "the School for Life" that was needed, and when he voiced his opinion to the Crown Prince, later to become King Christian VIII, the latter suggested that he put his ideas in writing. The present essay is Grundtvig's response to this challenge. Later as King Christian VIII issued a writ concerning the foundation of a high school at Sorø in accordance with Grundtvig's ideas. The King, however, died soon after (in January 1848) and the plan for a school was never carried out by the Folketing, the parliament introduced in 1849. In 1844, however, a folk high school had been founded at Roedding in Schleswig, and in a speech to a big political meeting Grundtvig publically welcomed it as a sign that the people of Schleswig wished to speak Danish and take part in political life in this language. The said folk high school became the first Grundtvigian folk high school in Denmark.

William Michelsen

The School for Life

The School for Death we know only too well, unfortunately, and not just those of us who went to the school that takes a pride in rest-. ing on the 'dead languages' and confesses that grammatical infallibility and lexical perfection are the ideal that the school, at the expense and sacrifice of life, endeavours to reach. No, with us the whole nation knows the School for Death; for that, without exception, is what every school is that begins with letters and ends with book knowledge, great or small, and that means everything that has been called 'school' over the centuries and everything that is still so named. For all letters are dead even if written by fingers of angels and nibs of stars, and all book knowledge is dead that is not unified with a corresponding life in the reader, and not only are mathematics and grammar soul-destroying and deadening, but so is all exhausting brain-work for man in his childhood, before his brain and the rest of his body are properly developed and before life, both the inner and the outer, has become so familiar to us that we can recognize it in description and can feel a natural desire to be enlightened about its conditions. Therefore, by seeking to implant in children the order, quietness, reflection and wisdom of old age, we graft only death from the weakness of old age on to both soul and body. We completely destroy the vitality of many of them, so that as half-grown boys they dwindle into mere shadows, and we work towards destroying human nature in all of them by defying its laws, so that even if the animal life in man survives, his experience of human life with us will in the very power of youth be that of an unnatural old man who in his diary can merely describe and curse his daily slavery under the yoke of animal nature. This is by no means just an obsession of mine, nor in any way just a sad observation by qualified philanthropic doctors, particularly in England and America, but also a pervasive truth that daily experience and every page in modern history reveal and confirm to every open human eye. The fundamental mistake to which our school-madness for boys' scholarship, or rather for the gods underground, can be traced, is, as the English doctors quite rightly observe, the opposition one imagines that exists between the body and the soul, so that what the body loses, the soul must win. Although this opposition has a little to do with Christianity as the conclusions that were drawn from it, nonetheless its letter and its shadow have undeniably served to sanctify both, inasmuch as after the school had laid us in the grave or at least deformed our healthy human nature and eroded our vitality, our fathers apparently consoled themselves with the thought that it was only the body that was being killed, only our completely depraved human nature that was being maltreated, and that as long as we had learned our catechism and our scripture as well as the next man, we had thereby obtained a title-deed to eternal life; and temporal death, far from separating us from it, was precisely the only road and desirable bridge to it. This superstition with a Christian appearance is now, I am sure, a long way from oppressing or comforting very many people in our time, but what our fathers ascribed to the sort of Christianity that can be learnt from books and forced into children is now generally ascribed to book-knowledge and mechanical reflection, so that they are supposed to be an everlasting gain for the soul, however useless or even damaging they may appear on earth to both body, and soul, to all the skilfulness that the life of man was predisposed towards, and to all the industry upon which our earthly welfare, cheerfulness and common sense obviously rest according to the will of providence and the nature of our being. Now wherever this unnatural partiality for death prevails, it surely does not seem very helpful to defend life in black and white or to enumerate the deadly sins of the school, but those of us who either by natural strength or particularly favourable circumstances retain enough human vitality to survive the illness and who see how the school works towards the destruction of the final remains of our glorious nature, so that all civilised nations must become slaves of their animal nature and of the barbarism around them, we cannot do other than testify, exhort and warn, first by speech and example as far as they go, and then by the pen, if for no other reason than to prove how dead and powerless are those letters for which people sacrifice the lives of their children and from which they expect eternal fruits. Nor is the position quite so desperate as it appears, and least of all in Denmark, where the so-called 'educated circles' are in fact more natural at heart than they seem or dare to admit to themselves; so here it will be a rare event if someone really wished himself or his children to die of education and literary skill. Therefore, at least among us speech and writing will doubtless gain sufficient acceptance and so to speak general applause, to Death's chagrin and in the interest of life, as soon as the people learn to realise its purpose; and the fact that this is very difficult must not surprise us, since both we who speak and write and they who listen and read, precisely because we are right in our allegation of the demoralizing influence of the dead school system, cannot help having a great lack of vitality and being bunglers of our mother tongue. The feeling that we lack and are in urgent need of a School for Life, as we have also recently learnt from the loud voice of this people in both Roskilde and Viborg[1] must be very common in Denmark; so that when nevertheless more schools for death are asked for, it is obviously and simply a mistake, which can easily be explained partly by the lack of a clear-sighted eye for life, which the demand for schools presupposes, and partly by the gullibility of the Danes who will invariably accept it as an article of faith when, quite unlike the grammar school, which itself professes its pact with death, a school boldly pretends to be the straitened way which leadeth unto life[2]. Therefore, the more we teach ourselves to speak and write naturally, clearly, plainly and cheerfully about this 'matter of life and death', the more the Danish and the living education, which we so much wish to replace the dead Latin one, will be understood and cherished. What makes the matter look desperate is obviously partly the genteel ambition of most Latinists both young and old, big and small, and partly the natural weakness of the Danes at logic. For genteel ambition resents the thought that a school education may not have been a giant stride forward to enlightenment but a step backward for life. Their weakness at logic, despite the strongest objections and everyday experience, easily dupes the Danes into believing that either in grammar or in mathematics a panacea is to be found which can cure it in the course of time, though by a method unintelligible to us. Obviously it is also absolute folly to believe that human nature, the life of a nation and its mother tongue would be able to win their case in a court thus constituted. But appearances deceive, and nowhere more so than in Denmark, for better or worse. So that just as here, contrary to our expectations, we have found many good things, so we will also find powerful spokesmen for nature, life, and the mother tongue, even if all the spokesmen should wear women's clothes! Yes indeed, on that we can and must depend, that Danewoman[3] and her daughters will soon learn how to understand us, even though we chatter away in a somewhat stilted and obscure way about life and about the definite advantages of resolute and vigorous industry and of a mother-tongue in all circumstances and in particular for 'everyday use', both in preference to mathematics and grammar, algebra, and lettering and all sorts of scholasticism; and when we have won over Dane-woman, then we have won the kingdom's immortal Queen since the King will never for long have the heart to refuse her anything. In fact then we have won Denmark's heart, which the head could never bear to crush. This, which since it has its own deep, natural reasons will be found to hold good more or less everywhere, is so completely and absolutely the case in Denmark as scarcely any-where else; so that here, when nobody else knows how a man is to be brought to see reason, his wife is sure to know, and among us there is hardly an old headmaster, much less a young teacher, that pretty girls could not easily teach to raise his mother tongue far above all dead languages. If only the woman here in Denmark realises that her language and all the enlightenment and education she can achieve, without learning either mathematics or Latin grammar, will under the old system be called coarseness and bar-barism, then the old system will lapse of its own accord. I see this with my own eyes every time my wife, despite my express prohibi-tion and my moving description of all the misery that can, and most likely, will follow, has cleared up and washed the windows in my study and compelled me so nicely to kiss her for it, whilst I scratch behind my ears and cannot deny that the room has become lighter and more attractive, and that the little things that can get mislaid are much easier to find than before, when everything was hidden in half-light under the dust and piles of paper. This is definitely what will happen to the studies inside the Danemen's heads, once Danewoman has courage to clean them up and wash their windows.

But is it not a form of treason to teach the admittedly fair, the kind, the captivating, the extremely ingenious at handling men, but nonetheless completely ungrammatical and unmathematical, un-scientific, that is inherently spiritless, unreasoning and barbaric sex to realize its power or at least to make use of it in this matter of education, which until now they have in all modesty allowed men to control? Is it not a blind physical power, and at that the strongest, most dangerous and most terrible we unite with to topple what we call a tyranny without having the least guarantee that it will not, in its blind activity, make bad worse and cast us headlong back into barbarism?

What I could and would say to this, if the fair sex we are talking about was not Danewoman and her true daughters, or if I was not just a little bit of a historian and nordic bard, I really do not know, but now the matter speaks for itself. For like all Denmark's serious poets I must thank Danewoman and her daughters for the fact that we did not have to emigrate like the North Americans[4] to find readers, and as a historian I would claim that those members of the fair sex who abused their superiority to the detriment of the spirit and of life, it was not they who wished to unite with me, not the friends of naturalness and the mother-tongue and useful industry, but precisely the opposite kind, whilst Danewoman bore, and her daughters garlanded both the heroes who defended the kingdom against all barbarians, the bards who in every land are the natural priests of the national spirit, and the saga-tellers who penned records that told of their heroic deeds. Finally it must be added that it is by no means because of a lack of valid arguments against the school that fights nature, the life of the people and the mother tongue that I feel the need of assistance from the fair sex, but only because the unreasonable partiality for what is unnatural, for book-wormery and for dead languages defies all rational argument and can only be defeated by another and stronger natural love that sets life high above books and which is at one with the mother tongue. Only to show this, only to ensure my alliance with Danewoman and her daughters, to show the innocence of it and the beneficial consequences that the victory it promises must of necessity entail, only for this reason, and not in any way out of confidence in the effect of rational argument in the present circumstances, will I endeavour to show the necessity of a national civic high school for the people, which, far from spiritually outlawing Danewoman and wounding her deepest feelings, will appeal both to her head and to her heart.

I shall first attempt to state as clearly as possible what I understand by the School for Life since I have noticed that the majority have not only rather vague, but actually very wrong notions of such an institution, which unfortunately only exists at present as an idea and on paper, with the result that it is always believed to be a literary laboratory where the rules are enjoined and inculcated, after which one must correct, improve and, in fact, transform one's life completely, the beginning of which is naturally a decomposition, that is, a death. This typically German fancy that life can and must be explained before it is lived, can and must be transformed by learned heads, this fancy, which must turn all the schools it establishes into workshops of decomposition and death where the worms live well at life's expense, this fancy I completely reject, and I maintain that if the school really is to be an educational institution for the benefit of life, it must first of all make neither education nor itself its goal but the requirements of life, and secondly it must take life as it really is and only strive to shed light on and promote its usefulness. For no school can create a new life in us, and it must therefore neither destroy the old one nor waste time developing rules which a different and better life would supposedly follow, if such were to be found.

As human life in all its complexity may nonetheless be classified into three main branches – the religious, the social and the scientific – so could one imagine three sorts of Schools for Life, namely the church school, the civic school and the grammar school, which must naturally have the same diversity as the corresponding life in society. But since it was only the civic school they expressed the lack of at Roskilde and Viborg, that is the one I will dwell on here, and that is so much the better since it is the only one that can be common to us all. We can and must all become educated and useful citizens, Danish citizens, but obviously only a few at a time can become professors and scholars; and as long as we do not delude ourselves that the church school can create a religious and Christian life where it does not exist, then we must of necessity conclude that we have enough church schools just as we have enough churches, for wherever life is lacking, its enlightenment is completely superfluous. Finally we have too many institutions rather than too few, too large rather than too small, in which to educate our clergy and our professors, whereas we have none at all in which to educate Danish citizens, so that even if all our educational institutions were admirable, and suitable as well, they would be exceedingly inadequate so long as we lacked a high school for the national and social life that we must all take part in, and must furthermore regard as the natural root and source of all endeavours, so that if *that* life is disdained and neglected, all other education must be as dead in itself as it is deadening for the people and damaging for the kingdom.

I am well aware that this is a great heresy among the learned since the Latinists have to maintain that above all one must be on guard against Danish and all Danicisms if one is to become a good Latinist, and one must constantly get away from Danish barbarism to 'classical soil' if one is to be at home among the ancients. At the same time the mathematicians preach a pure scientific spirit that is really concerned with neither life nor death nor any sort of human activity and in itself is so universal and cosmopolitan in its application that it cannot possibly limit itself to any particular language or give special preference to the needs and interests of any individual nation or kingdom unless it is there that mathematics both pure and applied is given most study and widest scope. Without retracting my scientific heresy, which lies roughly equidistant from both creeds and proclaims the whole, great life of man and of the race, not excluding but embracing the life of the nations and the individual as the object and task of the true and living spirit of learning. I nevertheless wish here sedulously to avoid all learned controversy and only from my own position as a common citizen observe that the country and the people are very badly served by erudite men on their guard against their mother tongue, and not much better served by those who want everything to be measured and numbered. So they would do all countries a great service if they founded a 'Learned Republic' in New South Wales, or wherever else there is room, and either made Latin their mother tongue there or created a universal language in which they informed the world, by the first ship available, of their discoveries, be they in Latin grammar or pure mathematics or somewhere in between. They would doubtless have been given this advice a long while ago if people had not held the conviction that the dead languages, and particularly Latin grammar, were not only the source of all profound knowledge but also of the education that was desired for all state civil servants and required for the clergy, judges and so on and had not by now acquired the notion, to boot, that mathematics can perform miracles to improve and ennoble all social pursuits, whilst in passing it sharpens the intellect to explain absolutely everything.

Now to make this as short and as clear as possible I shall allow the fact to speak for itself as to whether the Danish clergy, judges and so on, in order to become competent civil servants in their field, have to plough through Latin grammar in their childhood and write innumerable Latin proses, and later at university, in addition to text books in mathematics, astronomy, physics, practical and speculative philosophy still have to be taught, in the case of the clergy, to translate and explain the New Testament in Latin, and in the case of the judges to apply Roman Law to Danish conditions and translate and understand Danish Law in Latin. I allow all this to speak for itself, because the good cause will gain nothing from using my pen to attack so deeply-rooted a prejudice. But I confess that it is my firm conviction that all puerile learning is a monstrosity, and that bookwormery, segregation from the people, disregard of the mother tongue, and an idolization of Latin literature, which is inimical to all nations and kings and consists of eulogies over tyranny and rebellion, are the most inappropriate childhood learning for Royal Danish civil servants that I can imagine!

But suppose now that I was utterly mistaken in thinking this, so that I myself had to thank Latin grammar and proses classical reading and Latin exegesis of the New Testament for my being able to become the sound Danish priest and patriot I fancy myself to be. Even so it is nevertheless obviously not through Latin grammar, proses and going to school that one comes to love Denmark or becomes familiar with the people and its mother tongue, so there is at least one gap in our system for educating Danish civil servants who are to have an active influence on the life of the Danish society and people, as especially the church and judicial civil servants must. This gap could presumably not be filled by anything less than a high school for the Danish national and social life, where the mother tongue was sovereign and everything was concerned with the King, the nation, and the land of our fathers. Furthermore, even if one were to claim that a close acquaintance with Latin, a language the total opposite of Danish, and a general knowledge Rome, that tyrannical enemy of kings and nations, was the best preparation for a preference for all things Danish and close familiarity with them, since contraries forced together throw one another into relief (opposita juxta posita magis illucescunt) nevertheless, it cannot be denied that it is a hazardous venture to stop halfway and merely trust to luck that a Danish culture will be the result, which will place Latin in its proper, hateful, and abhorrent light. For if that does not happen, we are obviously more unsuitable as Royal Danish civil servants the more we learn to write and speak Latin, and the more completely we have grasped and the more deeply we have acquired the Roman outlook, mode of thought, and way of speech, which are not just totally foreign to the Danes' nature, mother tongue, and environment, but are actually inimical to them. I myself have spent at least thirty years getting Rome and Latin out of my system to the extent that you can see and hear, and that in many respects with modest success even though I have really had nothing else to do and have seldom been idle. So if it should be found appropriate in future to let the Royal Danish civil servants take this dangerous Appian or Latin way round to the Danishness they least of all can do without, then the homeward journey from classical soil and the conversion from the Roman mode of thought and the Latin style must be made easier for them in every possible way if the majority of them, even with the best of intentions towards their fatherland, are not to remain alien to it and incapable of sharing, much less governing the life of the nation. If therefore a royal Danish high school should not be considered necessary for any other people in the kingdom it is nonetheless absolutely necessary for the time being for the Latinists born and bred, who, if the discharge of their office is to be beneficial, must both think and speak Danish, and love and know our native land and its constitution better than any, but for one thing they cannot do this unless they come into living contact and interaction at a high school with a number of their contemporaries who know only Danish but who from experience know a greater or smaller area of the fatherland, the national and social life far better than can be described in any book, least of all the Latinists'. Furthermore, future civil servants will have great need of such a living education in the mother tongue and of a living acquaintance with the people and the country, even when, as we hope will happen in future, they have received an elementary education which was in no way hostile to the Danish way of life but in the kindest possible way related to it. For even when we in the North come to reject civil servants who are Latin stylists, classical thinkers and Roman orators, as I sincerely hope and trust we shall, the elementary knowledge of the Bible and its original language that is expected of a priest, and the acquaintance with laws and decrees that is expected of a judge, will require a certain amount of book-work by way of preparation, which, when pursued with diligence at a young age always results in a certain self-conceit, an alienating stiffness, an erudite manner and an inflexibility which in themselves would make the interaction at a folk high school almost a necessity. If this is the case now with all the Royal Danish civil servants, who, in order to be proficient and genuinely useful, must be servants of the people as well as of the monarch, how much more is it the case for all those who wish to prepare themselves suitably for the higher ecclesiastical and temporal posts, which of necessity have a great influence over general and fundamental acts of government! How absolutely necessary it is for them to have a living knowledge of the people and the country as they now are, together with as clear a view as possible of what they have been and may reasonably become. This knowledge and this view are necessary at all times if they are not to misdirect the aspirations of the people and the interests of the country. In fact they are doubly necessary now and in the near future, since first the Roman Church and Papal Law for four centuries and then the Latin School and Roman Law for three have sapped the strength of the people, disheartened the life of the people, inflated and complicated the legislation, restricted the equally inalienable freedom of the King and the people, and damaged in us all both high and low the naturalness of our way of thought and the purity of our mother tongue, from which they will never perhaps quite recover. In such circumstances, where we cannot assess completely the damage that alien and hostile elements have done to the country, much less repair it in a moment or a generation even with the best will in the world. We can easily see that even if we limited ourselves to a consideration merely of the education of higher civil servants, a Danish folk high school where we endeavoured to make the interaction between the young people of the country as great and as living as possible, would still be absolutely necessary for a brighter future.

But if a Danish folk high school as royal, free and popular as possible is necessary for the education of civil servants, can it be less so for the great majority of the people who neither will nor can become civil servants but who must support them as well as themselves? That the root and branch of the nation, its tenants and freeholders great and small, its artisans of all kinds, its sailors and businessmen, need no other enlightenment or education than what they can gain behind a plough, in the workshop, at the mast and in the grocer's shop, that may be what barbarians and tyrants believe, but it was never the Nordic way of thinking among the kings or the people and never could be, because it holds true here more than anywhere that we are all of 'one blood', so that the same educational ability is to be found in the poor man's cabin as in the rich man's mansion. This natural equality, which is now to be found really only in the Nordic countries where no foreigner has forced his way in and enslaved the former inhabitants, we cannot cherish enough since it is capable of giving our love of the fatherland a greater depth and the education of the people a greater truth than would otherwise be possible. And even if our, on the whole, dismal history of education had no other bright spot, still it is undeniable that such a bright spot was the school that from the Reformation onwards and especially since 1660 liberated and, so to speak, ennobled the boy from the most wretched hovel so that he could have a chance to develop to the full and rise to the highest offices. So only just recently, for example, the son of a smallholder in Funen[5] became, not only our greatest grammarian, but one of Europe's greatest philologists, and if his philology lacked the life and spirit to vanquish all the temptations of grammar and dead alphabetic lore, then it was obviously only the Latin school that had weakened him. So if there were no other people under the sun who deserved a folk high school in their mother tongue there would still be the Danes, and if no other people could expect its government's solicitude for popular enlightenment and patriotic education, then the Danes would, whose paternal kings in this as in all solidarity with the people have long been the models that Europe wanted all kings to imitate. However, should there still exist the smallest doubt as to the Danish people being worthy of an education after its heart, or as to the Danish King's recognition of and paternal solicitude for this, then this doubt would be defeated if not gloriously then at least gladly by the free voice of the people that King Frederik the Blissful called forth in the ancient capitals of Zealand and Jutland[16]. For it is as clear as daylight that a widespread patriotic enlightenment is needed in our day to make the voice of the people confident and civilised, and it goes without saying that there is no request to which His Majesty would rather lend his ear than to the request for a folk and civic high school for Life. For it is the Age of the Intellect we live in, and that does not mean that people are now born with all the intelligence they need, but that each of us has a great urge to go by his own mind with the result that wrong-headed nations have never done so much harm

as they do now and will continue to do so if we do not make pro-
vision in time for a general education, especially in social matters,
that can gather most of the good brains under one hat, that is,
under the gold crown on the people's head that is the paternal
crown of the monarch. Such an education, however, will also be a
success to some degree wherever in Christendom it is diligently
promoted, and I am certain that nowhere will it succeed better
than here in the North, and hardly anywhere so completely as in
Denmark, which, comparatively speaking, is never disturbed by
great passions but has her hereditary enemies in the apathy and
gullibility, which will only leave the day to the enemy when education is neglected or is of the wrong kind. Now education is never
neglected in Denmark, comparatively speaking, but it has hitherto
clearly been on the wrong track as it made the mistake of attempting to teach all of us every bit of German knowledge about the
heavens and logic, and the civil servants also Roman knowledge of
the world, but no common sense about what lies nearest to us: about
our own nature, conditions in the fatherland, and what is best for
the common interest, which, after all, is not only what in social
terms is the 'one thing needful'[7], but also probably the only thing
the average Daneman is capable of understanding. It is no wonder
therefore, but a consequence, as logical as it is regrettable of the said
mistake that most people in Denmark feel and admit they have no
understanding of earthly, real-life and social matters outside their
own position, occupation, and branch of trade, and that nearly all
the so-called understanding of natural and social matters in general,
at least as practised in Denmark, is false. For according to the
traditional path we have taken it must as a rule be either the Roman or the German mode of thought about the nature of man, the
social conditions and the general good that we have endeavoured
to promote, which Daneman has usually been very poor at, and
when he has had great success, it has given rise to the most dangerous misconception. For even if the Roman and German mode of
thought had created as much accord and social happiness on their
native soil as history teaches us they created the opposite, they
would nevertheless amongst such an unRoman and unGerman people as the Danish have done nothing but damage. However, it is
only a little misery that such a wholly alien mode of thought about
natural and social matters has created compared with what it would
do and be bound to do from now on, misleading or defying the free

voice of the people if a living, natural, and patriotic education does not soon banish the alien way of thought amongst the majority and leave it powerless amongst the rest, that is, harmless from a social point of view. But in an Age of Intellectualism such a gentle and beneficial enlightenment must increase in Denmark by the law of nature as soon as the opportunity is made available, since all living understanding or understanding of life is nothing more that a feeling within us that moves into the light and becomes aware of itself, and when Danemen reach an understanding that corresponds to that feeling which the gentlest, most peaceful and most loyal nation has displayed over the centuries, what mortal would not envy the King of the Danes his good fortune, and who would wish to live and see good times and not want to live in Denmark! Where else in the world should it be either more immediately recognized or more gladly agreed that a nation's happiness does not rest, as nearly all foreigners think, on the fact that it legislates for itself, but on the fact that the Law is 'fair and proper'[8] and that the government has both the honour of making and the power to uphold such laws. Where else in the world, I ask confidently, should this important truth, so generally misunderstood in our time as to bring misery to nations and sovereigns alike, be more immediately recognized and more heartily agreed to than in the country where the people with keen awareness of its significance solemnly handled on to the King unlimited power for paternal use. And where else, I ask again, would it be more certain that an absolute monarch would take pride in using his absolute power in a paternal way by adapting all the laws and institutions according to the enlightened nature of the people and the general good; where more certain than in the very country where the people's nature is the life source of royal power and where the absolute monarch, after thousands of demonstrations of his paternal care, crowned the work by voluntarily electing the voice of the people to his council. Truly in Denmark, where the ear of the people was raised to the royal mouth and the royal ear was lowered to the mouth of the people, there are, with the one exception of a natural patriotic education, all the conditions necessary on earth for the greatest social happiness, so that such an enlightenment here must of necessity be to the honour and happiness of both the King and the people, provided Heaven adds its blessing. And where, I finally ask, can the effort towards a gentle and friendly education of the nature which God Himself has created and of the conditions which His providence has ordained one be surer of Heaven's blessing than where as in Denmark it descended visibly, and averted a thousand dangers and allayed all our misfortunes, while we strayed from the old Royal Road and groped either for what hung too high above us or for what was not worth owning.

At this point, mindful of Denmark's good earth and lucky star, I would prefer to end my consideration of our need for a folk high school, which would in no way have been less even if we had not had it in common with any other nation in the world, and of the bright prospects it would open up for a domestic and social happiness which, should it be found to be without equal will thereby become only the more inestimable. I would prefer to end in order to turn to the gratifying consideration that when His Majesty, who desires everything that can serve to make Denmark happy, ventures to believe that a royal Danish folk high school would serve that purpose, then at that very moment it is ours, admittedly very imperfect, as everything human on this earth must be at first, but yet real, with the capacity for total perfection. As I say, I would prefer to end now, but I dare not do so before I have expressed as kindly and frankly as I can, my convictions concerning the school curriculum for life which *appears* to have the voice of the people behind it even though it assuredly has both the nature of the people and the experience of history against it.

The school that I have in mind is the secondary Boys' School, which is just as strongly scientifically based on mathematics as the grammar school is based on the dead languages, a school which with a smile at the German professor's understanding of the welfare of society I would pass over in silence, were it not for the fact that this terrible workshop for the death of society seems to be vociferously extolled by the voice of our people as the School for Life that we needed, but which I have now been near despairing of. For no writer can feel more deeply than I the impotence of his pen when set against the voice of the people or what passes for it, so if this new secondary school did not stand in the way of the Danish folk high school I would much rather pretend that I had not seen it at all, and leave it to experience and the high school to correct the people's voice or clear up the misunderstanding. Now on the contrary, I simply have to endeavour to show that such a mathematics boys' school cannot possibly in any way take the place of the

Danish folk high school or achieve a single one of the latter's beneficial effects.

Confining myself to this point I wish only to remark in passing that if the grammar school for boys is inappropriate for intending professors and a great misery for practical civil servants, then the mathematics boys' school must be equally inappropriate even for intending professors and a great misery for industrious citizens. In passing I will only add that the damage a country suffers at the hands of perversely educated civil servants, however great that damage may be, is only a trifle compared with the misery of warped commoners, who either cannot be bothered to work or can only be bothered to read, do sums on a slate, draw figures and make logical conclusions. For it simply must be remembered that it will never do to split a nation up into nothing but professors, civil servants, and paupers, unless they can all literally feed on air. Finally, I wish only to point out in passing the unassailable fact that the English and every nation that has been successful in social industry and prosperity did not reach their goal by using mathematics boys' schools, but by using only what is incompatible with them: the desire for physical activity, a good grip on their practical work and a longing from childhood for an independent position, whilst the High Germans, in spite of their scientific ennoblement of the day-to-day pursuits and the branches of trade, have watched both their industry and their prosperity decrease and have seen the preference for safe positions at public expense, even if the living was to be sought in prison, spreading from day to day. For I am more than certain that if one could get on proper speaking terms with the Danemen no one would come to learn more easily the lesson that even if mathematics was for all other nations both Fortunatus's purse and the philosopher's stone and source of joy, it would still not be either of these things for them. But in the course of more than thirty years as a writer I have been completely cured of the delusion that one can talk to people by writing books, even if they are read much more than most of mine, and therefore I only point out in passing what may indeed be the chief concern of the 'precious few' but what may well to the majority here sound as double Dutch.

On the other hand it seems to me as clear as daylight that even if the mathematics boys' school should be just as admirable a roundabout way to industry in society as the grammar school was believed to be for civil servant efficiency in Denmark, it would nonetheless still be so only for those who passed through it, and that must without a doubt darken our eyes when we consider what so many mathematics boys' schools would cost that would just accomodate the sons of all our townspeople, whilst in the rural areas the majority still remains, which is surely not to tarry in barbarism. It is equally clear, I believe, that however admirable a roundabout way to industry in society it might be to undergo the purgatory of mathematics, it was only so when the boys escaped intact, put all their sums and scientific demonstrations on the shelf, banged all the bookworm mentality out of their heads, put diligence on with their everyday clothes and eagerly got to grips with their respective trades. For if they did not, they were qualified at the very most to be professors of mathematics or teachers in schools of that sort, by which method we should acquire on a much larger scale a cycle just like that of the grammar school – of school attendance, examinations, getting a safe job – which must drain the resources of even the richest country let alone the poorest. Experience teaches, however, that it is no easy matter when one has spent or misspent one's childhood years in a schoolroom with books and slates, pen and ink and all sorts of high jinks, and in general led a sloppy, lazy life at the expense of others, to take hold of the hammer and tongs, axe and saw, or rope and tar barrels with eager energy, or generally gain proficiency in and feel happy with the so-called 'coarse work', the lower position and way of life, as regular as it is simple, which industry and prosperity in society demand, so I doubt whether even the best Danish folk high school will manage to convert the mathematics boys to promising young men in the practical social sense, and that it will be extremely necessary in such cases, is for me incontestable. However, suppose it was otherwise, suppose that by a miracle mathematics trained the boys in diligence, modesty and moderation, it would still hardly awaken or nourish their love of the fatherland, make them acquainted with the life of the people or add those years to their age which they must necessarily muster in order that they may reason with us about human nature and society in a way that is beneficial rather than harmful, so that when one had been through the mathematics school as a boy, one would still greatly be in need of a folk high school in one's youth, and in fact would usually need it very badly since the more one strives to develop a boys's reason the more one produces and encourages a self-opinionatedness and misunderstanding of real life, of which in his limited experience he is ignorant.

Nevertheless, I might as well break off now, since however crystal clear all this seems to me, who with a strong Nordic bent have endeavoured for thirty years to get rid of the whole, foreign, artificial way of thought, my pen is all the same unlikely to make it clear to the reading public, who are deeply imbedded in the Roman way of thought, usually without noticing that it only has coherence when one regards the 'educated people' as a flock of Romans who have all the rest of the world as slaves and are completely useless to a nation without slaves who must eat their bread with sweat on their brows and can only afford to support civil servants and intellectuals if also their lives and efforts contribute to the general good and will only have a mind to do so in the Age of Intellectualism when general education of the people will continue to improve their appreciation of society and weigh up against one another the advantages and difficulties of the various occupations while they gain an education that ennobles them and enchances even the lowest. These days we shout ourselves hoarse for freedom and education, and that is indubitably what we all are in need of, but the proposals for these things all have the same fundamental flaw in them as Plato's Republic, where the guardians of freedom and education themselves swallow up both, so that the people, for all their hard work, are given only the shadows of all the virtue and all the beauty to embrace, but are in fact given proud tyrants to obey, to feed, and, if it can be of any comfort to them, to admire and idolize.

Notes

1. Grundtvig refers to the advisory assemblies mentioned in the introduction p. 65.
2. Matthew 7.14.
3. The Danish equivalent of Danewoman contains a pun with Danish and a homonymous word meaning honourable.
4. Grundtvig refers to Washington Irving's long sojourn in Europe.
5. Rasmus Rask (1787-1832) is a Danish scholar of languages who was the first to draw attention to the Germanic sound shift (1814) and who is recognized as one of the founders of the comparative study of languages in the 19th century.

6. Grundtvig refers to King Frederik VI of Denmark.
7. Luke 10.42.
8. "Fair and proper" is a quotation from the preamble of the medieval Jutlandic Law.

V

Selections from
Within Living Memory

In the spring of 1838 Grundtvig was invited by a group of young men, mostly students of Copenhagen University, to give a series of lectures on the history of the past fifty years, that is the period from the time of his childhood (he was born six years before the French Revolution) up to the year 1838. On obtaining a royal permission Grundtvig began his talks on 20th June 1838. He lectured during the following weeks (apart from a recess from the middle of July to the beginning of August) on Mondays, Wednesdays and Fridays finishing on 26th November. The lectures were given at one of the residences of Copenhagen University, Collegium Borchianum. The audience grew from about 300 to about 600.

In the early 1830s Grundtvig had begun work on his handbook of world history, which, however, he never brought up to date. The lectures, Within Living Memory, may be seen as a draught for a final volume of the handbook, all the more so as Grundtvig had prepared notes for all 51 lectures. All the same, it does not appear as if it had been Grundtvig's intention to have the talks printed. The individual chapters were, as regards their manner and style, aimed at oral delivery. They gave him the first great opportunity of testing his teaching theory about "the living word" as a means of lively and rousing communication.

The great success of the lectures confirmed his belief in a major Danish people's high school (a kind of adult education university) located at the small town of Sorø in Zealand where history, particularly the history of the fatherland, was to be given a predominant position in the curriculum.

After Grundtvig's death his son Professor Svend Grundtvig, the eminent folklore scholar, published the manuscript of the lectures. They show Grundtvig's grasp of his subject matter, particularly in his description of the development of the French Revolution, but what retains their value are the personal judgments he makes and the visionary and poetic character he as a poet was able to give his words.

The lectures reflect important changes in Grundtvig's view of history and society. His preoccupation with the history of the French Revolution and its consequences (which is the central theme of the talks) changed his ideas about the position of Christianity in modern secularized society and under new political conditions and started him on the path towards unconditional acceptance of democracy and its institutions.

As a young man he had been a champion of absolutism and Lutheran orthodoxy, which determined his view of history and man. Now he admitted that the long dormant inclination to taking an active interest in the good and bad fortune of society was a positive value although he feared a development that might end in arid criticism. Nor was he convinced of the wisdom of the revolutionary demand for equality. Of freedom, on the other hand, he was an advocate and in particular of religious freedom since in his view Christianity does not stand in the way of realizing "the Christian human ideal" in the life of society.

Departing from an optimist view of the future – not least regarding the future of Denmark – he had gained courage to speak of the immediate past since he saw it as his aim to rouse and encourage "a higher and more living view of human nature in its historical development and of human history in its natural setting". Formerly a student of the remote past of man (the heroic age and the Middle Ages) he now realised that he belonged to the present day and that the Revolution's ideas about "universal freedom and complete naturalness" could and would lead to "a comparatively glorious and happy future".

The lectures Within Living Memory are as all his works highly subjective, a personal reckoning and a revaluation of earlier standpoints. What remains as a constant theme in the book as a heritage from earlier stages of his development is the hope for the survival of Christianity, the love of the fatherland and last, but not least, his permanent preoccupation with the human condition.

A heritage of his romantic youth is the idea of the historical mission of individual nations, the tasks allotted them by Providence in the progression of history. Grundtvig's coming to terms with the present had clarified his view of the divine mission of individual nations, the role they are going to play (and the one most of them have already played) in the course of history.

There were three European nations which Grundtvig loved and

admired: The Greeks, the English and the Norsemen, in particular the Danes. Conversely he entertained a permanent aversion for the Latin nations, the ancient Romans and the revolutionary French, and in addition he disliked the Germans, especially the Prussians who kept the Roman spirit alive, not least by their predeliction for military power.

In his lectures Grundtvig explains his ambivalent but mainly positive attitude to England and the English with whom he became more closely acquainted during his visits to the country in the summers of 1829, 1830 and 1831.

His observation of "the spirit of industriousness" in England makes him hopeful of a fruitful give-and-take between England and Scandinavia when materialist England becomes aware of its Norse spiritual heritage.

Behind this view of the future (which may be glimpsed in the preface for his Norse Mythology (1832)) there lurks an idea that had struck him as early as 1810: the seven churches mentioned in the Apocalyse reflect the course of history as far as each church corresponds to the seven "principal nations" which, according to Grundtvig, shape world history from the birth of Christ to the Day of Judgment.

Each of these nations was to have a period of 300 years when they dominate the development for better and for worse. The Greeks, for example, advanced whereas the Romans (and the Germans) thwarted progress. According to Grundtvig his day saw the end of the period of the fifth Church of Sardis, which Grundtvig identifies with Germany (running from the time of Luther to the age of Grundtvig). Now the age of the Sixth Church of Philadelphia was imminent being an age of brotherhood, goodwill, harmony and hope for the future. Grundtvig did not doubt that this Church was that of the North in the widest sense, including the English, as the inheritors of the Norse heroic spirit. The lectures, Within Living Memory, may be seen as an attempt to give a rational basis for this utopian historical vision.

Gustav Albeck

Selections from Within Living Memory

1. *Learning Exists for the Sake of Man*

July 6th

Well, gentlemen, it is ridiculous, but true and may very well be tragic that we so-called educated people are everywhere educated not to practise a stronger, nobler, and gentler life and language than the common multitude, but to offend and provoke them and to exalt ourselves above them and above one another. We are educated never to ask what we ourselves have done, or can and will do, but always what others have done or what in our opinion they ought and must do, without caring in the least how impossible it would be for us if we ourselves tried to do the same. This is what we call developing our minds and sharpening our wit, and, in fact, there is some truth in that. Learning has achieved a great deal through this form of education and will continue to do so until the endless critical scholarship drains man of his vitality, thereby setting free the unquenchable animal desire.

Then, of course, it will be all over for learning, reduced to a more plaything of the impotent spirit and held in contempt by carnal vanity. This was the way it went in Greece and Rome and it must be the way it will go in the new world as in the old because the laws of human nature can no more be changed or defied with impunity than other laws of nature. It must be the way, I say, if we cannot learn from the irreparable damage done partly to others and partly to ourselves whilst it still can be made good.

However, that I know we can do and shall do. Therefore it is no longer in despair, but with great hopes for the future that I now look back on the past and divide my attention between the good signs and the bad telling what I see and doing the little I can as I take comfort from the proverb: many a little makes a mickle.

You may well say, gentlemen, that at this point I myself is doing nothing but criticize, and you would be right; but if by doing so, I have taught just one of you that it is a bad failing, which for our own sake we must endeavour to correct, then I would have done much more than merely criticize, even though it may be at my own expense. However, I have come so far that I do not take it too much to heart, so long as I can make my contribution to the common good and make general this insight: that just as bad as it would be for all our doctors to be trained only to dissect, and to practise this skill on their patients while still alive, equally wrong would it be if in the world of the spirit we were educated and worked only to the same end. Consequently, the little advantage that learning gains by it is not only made at the expense of human life, both in ourselves, in society, and in all human relationships, but at so heavy a cost that only by turning down another road can we avoid bankruptcy. That is how I have escaped it, and that is the way I wish every nation to escape it, and that is how I hope at least my native land will steer clear of it. So I seize every opportunity to point out to you the obvious but forgotten or neglected truth that learning exists for the sake of life, human life, and must be neither practised nor promoted at the cost of life, but only in its service, for its enlightenment, and to its advantage, clarification, and embellishment instead of as now being generally employed to make life dismal for both ourselves and others, eroding its strength and distorting its true nature. Of this I must speak, and the only fault about it, which possibly ought to be avoided, is that I alone do the talking so that there is no live exchange of ideas between you and me. But that is also a result of our perverse education and scholarship, which never aimed at anything that improved life, but at producing by word of mouth or pen artistic tricks that people might like to dissect, or wrangles and literary feuds that might be diverting at our stage of development, just as bullfighting and cockfighting were at another. I am therefore not in the least afraid to say that I would regard all my talk about society and man's great problems as being a waste of time, if I did not contribute to the living dialogue on the subject, which alone can profitably shed light on and clarify the ideas.

2. The Advantages and Disadvantages of Revolution

July 13th

I never thought that the fifth act of Louis XVI's tragedy would be so difficult or rather impossible for me to tell, since it is full of moving incidents, and however much appearances may have deceived, Louis nonetheless dies evidently more royally than he lived.

But as I was reproaching myself for my shortcoming, I recalled an episode from the same act that made me realize what sort of a task it was that was beyond my strength.

After the Tuileries had been stormed for the first time (on July 20th) the legislative assembly sent some members up to express their sympathy to the Royal Family, and as the Queen herself was walking round with people from the castle and complaining about all the destruction the mob had caused, she noticed that tears had risen to the eyes of even the intransigent Jacobin, Merlin of Thionville, so she said to him, 'I see that you too cannot but weep to see how brutally the King and his Family are treated by a people he always wanted so much to make happy.' 'Yes, Your Majesty,' answered Merlin, 'I weep for your ill fortune as a beautiful, sensitive woman and housewife, but you must not think that I have a single tear for the King or Queen.' This was really such a rude thing to say that one must realise that Merlin was a Belgian before one can understand how it could be said to a beautiful queen in French. But as a historian I found that when I wished to relate the sad fate of these crowned heads, it was my task to do so in such a way that I would be heard to regret that Louis and Marie Antoinette, who in another situation would seem to have been a happy, lovable couple, should have been crowned to such an ill fortune, and to deplore the country whose Tree of Freedom, as one of the blackguards said, could only grow in royal blood, but not to deplore that such a horrible monarchy as the French ended as it deserved. This task I found too heavy to fulfil, and since I could neither narrate so serious an event with French levity nor present Louis as a martyr for the good cause, I felt that I had to give up completely all narrative and just point to both sides.

Now, gentlemen, you can hardly doubt that I am willing to let kings, and queens, even in France, be given their due with justice and fairness, since if you call me an *ultra*, it is bound to mean royalist; and that I possess the modicum of courage that may be required for professing one's royalism in Denmark that you surely do not doubt either. But nobody knows my view of the matter except me, and I shall endeavour to give you it as briefly and clearly as I can, since I think that both sides actually have a very distorted view of it.

I regard the democratic equality which the French aimed at in the revolution as a mirage that neither can nor should be found in society, and if it were, it would be as deformed as a body made only of hands, or, as the hydra was depicted, only of heads. However there is not only equality before the law under which the Almighty judges us all without respect of persons; there is also a parity according to the laws of human nature which history must take into consideration so that we are equally fair in our demands on human nature, whether it shines on the throne or goes unheeded in the cottages. Monsters is therefore what history calls Louis XI and Louis XIV as well as Marat and Robespierre, and fixes the same inscription on the altar of the idol of royal absolutism as on that of democratic absolutism with its horrible multitude of sacrifices. So it is not the French Revolution alone but the whole history of France over thirteen centuries, which one must pray that heaven will preserve itself and every society from; and that is the great truth that must be proclaimed and repeated again and again. To the same degree that other princes have imitated French kings must they be prepared for their subjects to imitate those of Louis XVI.

And whilst it is a comforting historical truth that the French extremism is only to be feared in those countries where the royal family tree, as in Rome, was the shaft of a spear, and where the people's tree of freedom will therefore be a spiked stick, as in Paris, even so there are everywhere princes and peoples making unreasonable demands on each other. This creates bad blood and if left unchanged, will lead to disaster, which would be very sad even if it were a much more humane one than the French. Unintentionally Christianity has drawn a veil over this mutual lack of moderation which it is very much the duty of its apologists to remove, and therefore I shall endeavour to show where the mistake lies.

For if both people and princes regarded their mutual relationship in a perfectly natural way they would not, especially now that light is dawning on history, make inflated demands on one another; but with Christianity a far higher human ideal has come into the world with the testimony that it can be realized by every nation and in all corners of the world. And both princes and peoples throughout Christendom have made it an occasion for raising mutual demands that cannot possibly be fulfilled, inasmuch as the princes demand of their subjects, and the subjects of their princes that they be the perfect Christians in the flesh that the New Testament describes, that is, demigods in spiritual power and wisdom, humility and meekness, be lions and lambs, heroes and martyrs, all according to circumstances or as required.

That Christianity is now completely innocent of these mistakes would have been seen long ago if both princes and peoples had maintained a true freedom of religion. For then it would have been apparent that there are relatively few people anywhere who would so embrace Christianity as to make it a new principle for their lives, and one would never have expected Christian heroic strength of those who had not even reached Christian innocence. But then princes and peoples forced each other to be addressed as Christians and the priests made them believe that it helped if not here then hereafter, and thus the ideas have become so muddled as they have in the eighteenth century that even those who, like Frederik the Great, Rousseau, Voltaire and all their idolizers, explicitly refused to be regarded as superstitious slaves and idiots or mean hypocrites and impostors, which in their opinion all Christians must be – even they, however, demanded Christian perfection of one another and of the whole world. So the difference was only that they claimed it was the Christian faith that up to that point had prevented the Christian ideal of man from being realized in the secular society, which otherwise would soon happen if one just got rid of faith. Yes, gentlemen, it is absolutely ridiculous, and yet it is a fact, that the apparently unchristian and ungodly French court demanded that the people should perform and endure all that Christ's apostles alone could and would, and that the Parisian mob and its leaders for their part demanded the same of Louis XVI and all the other authorities

Therefore, wherever social relationships are indeed to be reborn and gain stability, Christianity, as a force quite free and incalculable, must be left completely out of consideration, remembering that the human ideal it has brought into the world, but seldom realized in convincing form, can still less be realized without it. One must stick to the human nature that history in any particular place reveals as that which decides the yardstick for the reasonable demands people can make on one another and creates the natural ideal which society can endeavour to realize there successfully. Then princes and people will not torture themselves and one another by guarding against every possible abuse of power and freedom, but strive to promote and facilitate the best use of them, which, being the most beneficial, both profits us best and makes the gross abuses of them as rare and bearable as such deeds rightly branded and severely punished as gross crimes always have been in a well-organized state. Then it will also be realized that, properly understood, the freedom of the King and the freedom of the people, far from being incompatible, actually need each other much more. So it is mere illusion for them to believe that one side's gain is the other side's loss, since it is always only some beast of prey or other – calling itself the nobility, the clergy or what you will – that wins what they both lose. Thus, when mutual freedom and the good order which springs from it are recognized for what they always were, namely, the legal foundation of society, then great days will dawn, not so much perfect days, which are socially impossible for citizens on this earth, but real days, like the great days of every nation, and so much the more beautiful, as popular enlightenment and a natural education cannot help making them.

With these bright prospects I wish to thank you, gentlemen, for the attention you have hitherto accorded me, and to beg your attention during the continuation of my talks on the demands and signs of the present age. For I told you at the outset that only because I see bright prospects, especially for this plot of earth we call our own, this plot of earth which down the ages has never been the spoil of foreigners and will therefore never become a battleground for rebel slaves and effete tyrants, but a sanctuary like the Æsirs'[2] famous Place of Assembly under the ancient ash, where they spared even the Fenris Wolf[3], so as not to defile the tree with blood – only because here I see bright prospects which need only historical enlightenment to develop and reveal themselves in all their glory, as our lovely country this summer eve needs only the morning sun to delight our eyes – only for this reason and in the hope of being able to give especially my younger countrymen a brighter and better founded hope for the future than they usually seem to me to entertain, only for this reason did I decide to speak in public about the past, and chose as a sample by no means the part of history I have loved the deepest and cultivated the most diligently, but precisely that part which for a long time I have scorned and as far as possible have ignored. I chose the most recent period of history because it is closest to us all and therefore makes the strongest demand on general attention and offers the clearest insight into the human life that we all share.

I said at the outset that I realised it was a daring venture and I repeat that this seems very much to be the case. But that was in my honest opinion the best I could do, so I am pleased still to have found the courage to attempt what cannot possibly be posterity's loss and may be something of a gain. And if my talks on more recent history, on the history of the nation at the moments when it fused with my own, can help to awaken and nourish a brighter and more living view of human nature in its historical development and of the history of man in its natural setting, I shall not only be content for my talk to be called in all other respects unskilled work, which from now on will not be tolerated. But my triumph will be precisely that posterity finds it so and replaces it with masterpieces; because I know it is unskilled work, whether it is considered so or not, and I only find it bearable because I hope that I myself will gradually be able both to improve it a little and above all to arouse the younger generation to make it a lot better, to climb on to our shoulders, as is their calling, and see further, learn from our mistakes and profit from them.

It is not out of modesty, gentlemen, that I speak thus. For whether it be illusions or reality, I really do believe that I can speak just as clearly and lucidly about human matters as any of my contemporaries; but I realize it is unskilled work with all of us we are bunglers in our use of the mother tongue, bunglers in our history lectures, bunglers in the way we serve our audiences so long as we just talk and fail to understand how, through a living dialogue, we can initiate and sustain the general participation and interaction that is the life blood of the High School and the condition for progressive enlightenment. To this may be added, as I remarked, the fact that I have scorned and ignored more recent history, and have done so for natural reasons, so that I cannot move around in it nearly so freely, nor express myself nearly so spiritedly as I can in classical or medieval history – I say for natural reasons because as an individual I am of a historical-poetic nature, finding it easy to enthuse over the eagle-flight of the human race in its poetic youth and over its giant strides in its proper historical manhood, and consequently I am prejudiced against its snail's pace in the present, which seems to me to bespeak only an impotent, cold, mean-spirited old age – in a higher sense as unhistorical as it is unpoetic.

Even the revolution and its consequences, to which I would not deny a certain greatness, therefore seem to me to be a fearsome proof of the impotence and spiritual poverty of the race that acclaimed a

monster, half animal and half devil, as its saviour[4]. So it was not until I joined the quiet in the land that I discovered that the present
also has a historical-poetic side from which it can be regarded, and
once it is, will come to stand in its proper light and become what
it was obviously appointed to be – one of the great periods of
transition between a past without hope and a future full of hope,
with a glorious flowering. Now for the first time I saw that we,
who arrogantly rose above the present with its low, prosaic view
of all human relations, its philistine interests, its puerile search
for freedom and its self-conceit, that we, I say, stood in the way of
a better future just as much as those who idolize the present, and
that we would therefore do well to remember that we ourselves, with
all our lofty opinions, belonged to the present that we so deeply
despised and so bitterly railed against, and that we repaid only with
ingratitude the age that begot and bore us and would deserve
only the ingratitude of posterity if we wasted our strength on glori-
fying the past, which has irrevocably disappeared, while supressing
the present, which alone can accomplish anything, since it alone
holds the last hope of the human spirit and is only to be abandoned
in despair.

Then I set about regarding my times as closely and impartially
as possible and whole heartedly involving myself with everything in
them that prophesied a better and a happier future, better and
happier not just for individual poets and scholars, not for individuals or classes, by whatever name they are known, but for the ordinary run of people and for the full development and clear enlightenment of our profound and wonderful nature, which is obviously the Creator's will and the inclination of the human spirit.
Then I found, to be sure, neither the present in all its aspects,
nor the French freedom and enlightenment which it idolized and
still does idolize somewhat, to be beautiful and joyful, much less
heavenly, but found, however, traces of what is essentially human
even in the middle of Paris, and found that the tendency to general
freedom and radical naturalness that the revolution points to, can
and must lead to a relatively glorious and happy future, where
human nature is a little better and deeper and therefore freedom is
nobler and more unassuming and the enlightenment more thorough
than in France. To be sure, I find great difficulty in suddenly having to make such a concerted effort to catch up the arrears in my
closer acquaintance with my times, and even greater difficulty in

being truly impartial lest, for fear of the opposite, I seem partial towards what is wicked, and the greatest difficulty of all in becoming engaged sympathetically with French history, which, like everything French, I find repulsive. But I have struggled with these difficulties as best I can and am still doing so, so just as long as you, gentlemen, do not lose patience, I very much hope to conquer them, so that at least my young fellow-students will realise they can be overcome when, like those, one has a mind to do so and time on one's side.

Therefore, gentlemen, although I appear to have most of my life behind me I nevertheless do have a mind for something, a mind, if I can, to break through the ice not just to a truer appraisal of the past and the present but also to a freer relationship and a more lively exchange between the old and the young, which is the condition for all true freedom and all profound historical enlightenment. To a degree I owe this 'mind' to an old myth which is not even Nordic; the great Eastern myth about the Phoenix, which may only have come to us in scraps from Greece and Rome, but which in my eyes has been as exceptional of its kind as Fidias's masterpieces were of theirs, so just as art connoisseurs rate the scraps from the Parthenon above a complete work of art by Thorvaldsen, so do I rate the handing down of the scraps of the phoenix myth above the best poem by Oehlenschlaeger[5]. For in these scraps I have found the human spirit's own ideal of its great destiny expressed with confidence, magnificence, and life. I presume you all know this, gentlemen, but I do not know whether you have noticed the little feature which particularly encourages me and which I think should encourage us all, and I cannot use this moment better than to remind you that this Phoenix, which every morning in its earthly paradise greeted the rising sun with heavenly song, is the symbol of the human spirit in its highest flight and most natural activity. And when the myth says that after a thousand years of life this bird built itself a nest in the palm forests of Syria of the most spicy fragrant plants on earth and burnt to ashes with it, kindled by the pure rays of the sun, this clearly depicts to my eyes the Middle Ages – the age of glowing hearts, wonderfully fiery and fragrant but also wrapped in clouds of smoke emptying itself out and wasting away. So when the myth ends with the ashes being rolled together into an egg, from which the sun hatches a living creature, first, to be sure, in the form of the smallest worm, but then nevertheless growing and developing from the morning dew into a bird in its father's likeness, with his voice and with the right of inheritance to the beautiful fatherland, to which, fully-grown and accompanied by all the birds of the forest it returns in joy and triumph, I cannot but see in this an image of modern times as encouraging as it is striking, in which learning up to now was undeniably a bookworm that only wanted to gnaw on the momuments of the beautiful song of the Bird of Antiquity, and therefore found only its eagle claws worth envying, but nonetheless claimed to have been called to resemble him in everything and to be heir to all his demesne. However ridiculous therefore this claim sounds in the mouth of a bookworm, I nevertheless came to believe in its validity through the way the prophecy had hitherto been exactly fulfilled, and I thought I could feel within myself how the worm began to be transformed into a tiny bird. And since that time I see this change taking place wherever the spirit was present in olden days, and I consider my attitude to you now, gentlemen, to be just such a transformation through which the bookworm endeavours to shed its skin. This can, of course, be difficult enough to achieve and at times somewhat boring to watch, but if, as I hope, the result is a little bird that can learn to sing, it will be to our mutual delight.

3. On Germany and the German Spirit

October 26th

This evening, gentlemen, I am supposed to be informing you about Teutonism, properly speaking, as it whistled and roared about our ears in the years 1815-20;[6] but to keep my conscience easy I must first of all remind you that I have a reputation for being almost as bitter an enemy of the Germans as of the Romans, of the holy as of the unholy Roman Empire. And since, according to the proverb, there is no smoke without a fire, I myself presume that in this matter as in many others I am somewhat lacking in historical impartiality.

However, you must not believe that it is bad as many of my books may conclude, partly because one often reads somewhat superficially and partly because I have found it unwieldy for everyday use to weigh all my words in a balance. Firstly, there is no question of my hating the Germans as people, but only of an incompatibility with the way of thinking which on the evidence of experience comes most naturally to the Germans. Secondly I believe that among the Germans there may and have been far better people than myself. And thirdly I think that Germany has of late deserved much credit for the freedom and the enlightenment of Europe. So all in all, the Germans will hardly find anywhere outside Germany and Denmark where there is less anti-German feeling than in me.

My whole quarrel with the Germans is really concerned with the fact that they are determined either to make me a German, or to regard me as a fool; and I give as good as I get and do not wish to be either. Instead I assert that Denmark is no more the tail of Germany than the Norse spirit is a sprite serving the Imperial German reason. On the contrary, it is a sovereign entity, which has performed a multitude of great deeds that German reason could not emulate, and which will continue to do so.

Incidentally I am willing to admit that everybody can be good in their own right; but German reason has so far not been satisfied with that; this is why we are at war over Denmark and the Norse spirit, and time must decide who is right, for in the world of the spirit the stronger will always prevail.

Germany deserves much credit for freedom and enlightenment in modern Europe and consequently mankind is greatly indebted to her, a fact that we must always proclaim and appreciate, whatever else we dislike about the German mentality, in particular its influence on our situation, which always results in us violating our own nature, and that is anything but German.

Denmark's ancient quarrel with Germany is also purely a question of freedom and independence, which the Germans simply cannot accept since they have got it into their heads once and for all that Denmark does after all belong to the German empire, thinking and speaking Low German just like Holstein, and should therefore just like Holstein politely agree to think and speak High German; and it is to no avail what argument you draw from history or nature in our defence.

Just as Emperor Frederick Redbeard in the 12th century attempted to force our Valdemar the Great to recognize him as Denmark's feudal overlord, so do German letters of the 18th and 19th centuries also attempt to force us into admitting that, in spiritual terms, Denmark was a province of the Holy Roman Empire which might well rebel against Teutonism in its language and mentality, just as the old Danish kings did against His Imperial Majesty, but which could never have the right to secede, and could never again anything but disgrace by doing so.

No matter how much we implored the stern judges to consider that we are not usually even capable of pronouncing *sich*, let alone understanding the German philosophers, we still got the answer that it was our own fault, that it was the fruits of our disobedience, our softness and lack of proper discipline, and that furthermore all our objections, being solely derived from experience, and therefore only empirical, could not shake the rational deduction they had made: namely, that just as all the Romance languages were merely corruptions of Latin, so were all the Gothic languages, which ought to be called Germanic, merely distortions of German.

And even though one might stretch a point in the case of the proud and strong mountain-dwellers in Norway and Sweden, one could not possibly allow a land such as Denmark, inwardly and outwardly as flat as a pancake, to stick its chin out and demand a status as high as the Scandinavian mountains.

This, then, is the relationship that Denmark, or at least I, have with the Germans; so I cannot of course pass for an impartial judge of their nationality or their national character. But then I do not wish to be a judge; I wish only to express my opinion as freely as any German expresses his, namely, that Europe must be glad that since time immemorial Germany has been so chopped up that, however impressive it may be, it is still split downwards and across. For if you consider all the heads that think and speak German, all under one hat, all under a German Emperor Napoleon, then it would be a power far more fearful in human eyes than France in her most dangerous period, and they would be far harder taskmasters in consequence of the fact that, to my way of thinking, they are far more serious and thorough.

October 29th

My last talk, gentlemen, was about the Age of Ghosts between 1815 and 1820 in Northern Germany when the whole nation apparently fought with its own shadow as if it was a mysterious power attempting to overthrow the old royal thrones and ducal seats in order to transform the whole of Germany either into a huge republic or into a similar empire. That it was a fight against shadows I concluded, correctly so it seems, partly from the fact that even with the Argus eyes of all the police and all the Inquisition they still could not discover anything apart from a few scraps of paper, on which someone with an hour to spare or in a moment of madness had drawn some nonsense – partly for this reason, and partly because even the use of wrong measures to quell the imaginary revolution at birth did not provoke even the slightest attempt at one.

If, however, such a revolution really had been brewing and it had been possible to crush it by declaring war on the German universities and German literature, then I would not have been the last to praise Prince Hardenberg's vigilance[7] and admire Prussian statesmanship. For I can no more find the least urge or call to take up the cudgels for German universities and catalogues of books than I would wish to live the day when the whole of Germany so-called, from the Baltic to the Mediterranean and from the Vistula to the other side of the Rhine should become a republic or an empire in more than name only, since even the tyranny that France under Napoleon perpetrated on Europe would only be a trifle against such a German tyranny under its war-god, which, I think, will not fail to happen. For in that respect nations will find German gravity and thoroughness ten times as troublesome as French frivolity and superficiality. And we poor Danes who have had enough trouble defending our little bit of individuality against a chopped-up Germany would as likely as not be swallowed whole when she is united.

It is obvious that such a political unity, which gathered all its forces into a monstrous German war-machine, would be no less destructive of all that is good inside Germany as of all that is outside; but it seems more than reasonable that the danger that threatens Germany and Europe is more likely to come from the military state of Prussia than from the German universities. So if it was in order not to be led into temptation that Prussia gave up her popularity and quarrelled with the German world of learning, then it was a self-denial, which must at the least make us excuse a great deal. But seriously, we and the whole of Europe must wish for each of the existing kingdoms, or at least the major tribes – the Saxons, the Franks and the Swabians – a constitution and a status after their heart's desire. For in this way enlightenment will make unbelievable gains and the peoples will balance out each other, so we shall only need the mouth and the pen to defend the border and to build a Dannevirke[8] where the entry is otherwise left unguarded.

For it is my firm conviction that the spirit must be free everywhere, and that it never endangers any state unless the latter violates what it cannot possibly control and what it therefore should at least be wise enough not to incite and embitter, just as there has never been a more unfounded fear since the world was created than the fear that the scholars of Germany, who were never able to agree on anything, not even on casting off the Papal yoke, should conspire against any government that, unlike Napoleon and his imitators, does not intend to annihilate all freedom of learning.

Finally the enthusiasm for the Age of Chivalry in the Middle Ages, which was what united a number of German students with Görres[9] at their head, undoubtedly had a very ridiculous side to it, which the students would certainly not allow anyone to laugh at. But young students with enthusiasm for nothing in particular will still booze and enthuse. And who would not much prefer them to enthuse about their great fatherland, which is the glorious field of the national spirit throughout the ages? And although I am far from idolizing Germany in the Middle Ages or extolling to the heavens as masterpieces of art the Lay of the Niebelungen, the Book of German Epics, and the Minnelieder, in which the age has engraved itself, it is nonetheless a thousand times worthier of a nation to overdo its admiration for the pleasing expression and unique chievement of its spirit than to despise and deride it. For the latter, which, while Latin held away, was the case in Germany far more so than with us, is spiritual death leading to beastliness, slavery, and national destruction. By contrast, the former is only the national bias which every nation, just like every man, has for what is his own, which is therefore to a certain degree inseparable from the vitality of the national life of any country. So the nations must learn to forgive each other for this bias, so long as it does not try to assert itself with real weapons. The Germans were never closer to doing justice to ancient and medieval Scandinavia than when they had a passion for their own antiquity; and for the simple reason that spirits always have a certain respect for each other, but the spiritually dead hold them all in contempt.

4. On England and the English Spirit

November 9th

Charles and Polignac[10] appear to have trusted Wellington; but for what reason I do not know. At any rate, their hopes were dashed when, just as the decrees were published on July 26th, William IV acceded to the English throne and immediately recognized Louis Philippe, dismissed Wellington and concluded an alliance with France. In this connection the growth and stature of England will have to be considered.

I suppose I am really what you would call a 'stay-at-home'; but I have been to England, and I must admit that I feel the same way about my trip from Copenhagen to London as Gert[11] felt about his from Harslev to Kiel: it was a trip I shall never forget. Whether or not as a result I have been stricken with what is known as 'Anglomania' – or in plain Danish 'gone mad on England' – what I would rather not quarrel about with anybody, just as according to Roman law all poets were condemned to the madhouse on the judgment of Cicero, the Oracle, who said 'All poets are mad' (non est poeta sine furore), but I shall endeavour to show you that one does not necessarily have to be mad to have, an unquestionably historical preference (among all the great powers) for England. I say 'among all the great powers' deliberately; for to be honest I prefer the small nations, and incomparably most of all our little Fatherland. But to confess to such an unquestionably historical partiality towards one's own is also something that the Danish people need to learn from the Englishman, who would unhesitatingly assure us, soberly and seriously, that even if England could not survive unless the rest of the world perished, he would still vote for old England (old England for ever).

You see, gentlemen, in every nation this must be the way of thinking and self-reliance of the citizens that will make them lead any life worth talking about; and it is a lamentable state of affairs when, as is still the custom with us, we cherish that basic principle at heart, but for fear of the Latins, the Germans and the moralists, we dare not stand up for it, we hide our unquestionable partiality towards our Fatherland, our mother tongue, and all that belongs to them as though it were a crime, and we waste our energy on an inevitably stiff, torpid and unsuccessful copy of something foreign that we do not love but often actually hate. – However, I point this out only in order to draw your attention to the fact that I have in no way gone *so* mad on England that I would prefer England to Denmark, or wish my Fatherland to be in any way anglicized, but that my first wish is that we should have the courage to be ourselves and show ourselves for what we are, and then to realise that of all the great powers England is the one, both spiritually and temporally, to whom we wish all the good fortune that can be consistent with the freedom of Greece and Scandinavia, and the one which we must compete with to the best of our ability by removing all the bounds that impede or encumber our living industry, and above all by considering what is useful and to our lasting honour.

Now, gentlemen, in most countries people work for fear of the rod, and in Germany industry is considered a virtue to be exercised for its own sake, which becomes purer in essence the less usefulness or enjoyment one obtains from it. But if one wishes to see people working solely for usefulness, one must go to England, and that is worth the trouble. For doubtful as it may be that this kind of industry is the one most worthy of man, so much is nonetheless certain; that it is worthwhile, and that it alone offers a fruitful interaction with human life and all its powers.

The free and living industry, gentlemen, that masterly grasp of what is beneficial, the clear eye for what is really and truly honourable, that was what I really admired in England, and what I am sure Denmark can acquire to a degree that very likely will not make us as wealthy and mighty, but still prosperous, independent, respected, and a thousand times happier than the famous Island Race, who derive little pleasure from their greatness, power and dominion because they love and are loved so little.

This, then, is an open confession of my Anglomania. And now to a consideration of Great Britain in the history of the world, where only in the latest sequence of events from 1788 to 1830 she has won an influence over the whole European family of nations, something that not even Russia, much less any other power, can pride itself on – a decisive influence which her out-of-the-way position on the map, her peculiar constitution, and in particular her disdain of the continent and the narrow-minded prejudices of the eighteenth century had delayed but could no longer prevent. *This* is the great political transformation which the revolution and Napoleon brought to Europe; that it is no longer France, Prussia, and

Austria, but England and Russia who hold the balance, so that what they can agree on nobody dare oppose, and what they quarrel about is actually which of them is to be the sole master. So here we have a land-power and a sea-power on a colossal scale, quite different from Rome and Carthage, when they met on Sicily; two world-powers who can really only clash with one another somewhere else in the world, in North America or the East Indies.

November 12th

Gentlemen, in my experience England is a boring country to be in if one has no house or home there or daily business to satisfy one. For everybody there, from the Prime Minister to the pickpockets, is so terribly busy with his own occupation, and the inns are so cheerless and the private houses so enclosed and fortified in every way that a stranger is either left entirely to his own devices, like an owl among crows, or he at once gets tired of seeing what an effort it takes and what a sacrifice it is for an Englishman to devote half an hour to him, let alone a whole hour. I have therefore never been closer to despair than when I arrived in England for the first time, which to some extent was undoubtedly due to the fact that I was already getting on in years when I first ventured out into the world, so to speak, and that I arrived, somewhat precipitately, having gone out of the Customs House here on to a Danish ship to disembark just like that at the Customs House in London, which could not help but seem to me like arriving as a perfect stranger in another world.

However, I conclude that the cause of my despair lay outside me rather than within me, or in my Danishness rather than in my being a bookworm, from the fact amongst other things that at one point I met in London a much younger, healthier and already much-travelled fellow-Dane who before he could get to work was so desperate that he believed that had it not been for his wife and children back home, he would have jumped straight into the Thames. I have also a strong suspicion that at the bottom of the tremendous English busy-ness there lies a good deal of despair. For they are in no way like the Germans, practising their industry as a virtue for its own sake. Work in general does not seem to give them any pleasure, and although self-interest is the most common incentive, one nevertheless sees many an Englishman who is just as busy rushing round the world as others are working, or who is just as busy wasting money as others are earning it.

But however boring I have generally found staying in England to be, I have found it equally pleasurable a country to think about since my return to Denmark, where people usually allow themselves plenty of time for everything, so that one can examine all that business at leisure and consider it from both sides, the bright as well as the dark. And the more I do so, the clearer it seems to me that we ought to want a good deal of this busy-ness for ourselves, even though Copenhagen will thereby become a far less agreeable place to live in for foreigners than it now has the reputation of being and undoubtedly is. For even with regard to foreigners, we ought to prefer them to say 'We were really bored to death in Copenhagen but we left with a picture of great and lively industry which we would not have missed on any account', than that they should say, as they usually do nowadays, 'Copenhagen is a very beautiful and entertaining city, but that is all there is to be said, since gastronomy and diversions seem to be the only things that are pursued with any energy and fervour'.

But forgive me, gentlemen! It was not about such trifles as Copenhagen and myself, but about great England and industry on a large scale that I should be speaking this evening, and I shall do so as best I can if only I knew how to begin a talk which must be brief and yet as far as possible depict an industry to which there is no end or beginning: a *perpetuum mobile*. However, your are presumably not expecting me to describe either the English factories or coal mines, the steamships or railways, bone manure and artificial methods of agriculture, of which I have seen very little and understood even less, and which furthermore, I assume, are explained at our Polytechnic Institute. Nor are you expecting a trade balance on imports and exports or an enumeration of incoming and outgoing ships, or an analysis of the exceedingly complicated affairs at the stock exchange and the English finances, be they private or public, the banking system and the Bank, the growing debt and the sinking funds; for they are partly something of a mystery to me and partly something we assuredly get enough of in our new secondary schools[12], and finally to my mind they are frightfully boring to talk about if one is not involved in them oneself.

But what is it I call the internal constitution of a country when it is not what every sensible person calls it? Perhaps I can best illustrate this, gentlemen, with an analogy. For if one asks an anatomist about the internal workings of a man, one naturally expects to hear all the intestines enumerated, discussed, and examined. But if one asks a philosopher, one will of course get quite a different answer; and although I may be no more a philosopher than an anatomist, nonetheless the internal workings of a country are for me the same as the internal workings of a man are for the philosopher, with the only difference that he speaks of faculties and life as such, whereas I as a historian speak of their manifestations in human pursuits and in society. What I just mentioned is only the tail-end of this, but I always prefer to start with the head, and will do so now, though England's is split in two down and across the middle as are the Crown and the Government and both Houses of Parliament.

How far this carving up of government is desirable for the people they themselves must know best, and no nation has boasted more of its constitution than the English from 1689 to 1789. But for any King who is competent at ruling I know full well this division must be intolerable; so if there is to be no trouble, either the King or the constitution must become a shadow, in which case the latter becomes very dangerous and the former a very expensive business amongst other things. So much for the division, which at so high a level as the head must be does not please me at all, however else the rest may be. But we must notice that the division is not the new-fangled French and German one, which in the course of these talks I have often had to refer to, that is, the separation between what we call the legislative, the judicial and the executive powers. No, the English division has its roots deep in the Middle Ages and blends these powers so masterfully that when their four claimants each take what belongs to them and stand their ground, then the trouble starts. For it is clear that the King can do nothing on his own apart from choosing his ministers, but he can change them as often as he likes and through them he can destroy everything that Parliament does; and one of them (the Lord Chancellor) is not only what we would call President of the Supreme Court but actually embodies the Supreme Court in his person. Turning to Parliament, it is able not only to overthrow all the ministers but to arrest and judge them — just not hang them. And if we then distinguish again between the Upper and the Lower Chamber, like the drawing-room and the sitting-room, then the Lower House cannot do much more on its own than grant or refuse to grant taxes. But even where money was far less of a driving spirit behind everything, one can easily see that in our day it has sufficient power to stop the whole machinery, if it wishes to do so.

Since on the other hand the King and the Ministers he selects both have the right independently to declare war and have command over the army and navy, they are naturally tempted, if they are proud and bold, to curb Parliament and if they are clever to pack it as we pack cards. So England only makes herself look a little ridiculous when she trumpets forth the wisdom of her constitution; for it is, as I have said, an old garment from the Middle Ages and no matter how well one patches it, it remains patchwork. And it is not even English in origin. It is Godfrey's[14] crown of thorns, which Richard Coeur de Lion brought home with him from the Holy Land without knowing it. He never wore it himself, but left it to his brother John Lackland, and the Papal Legate and the English barons joined hands to place it firmly on his head. To be sure, gentlemen, when one reads the history of the Middle Ages with due consideration, one sees that the new Kingdom of Jerusalem founded during the Crusades became the pattern for all the European kingdoms, where the three classes – the nobility, the clergy and the commoners in various combinations constituted a state council which endeavoured as far as possible to usurp both the royal power and the voice of the people, so the kings became shadows and the peasants became slaves. And although the English state council was for a long time curbed by powerful and tyrannical kings, it nevertheless reached its goal, later admittedly, but more completely than any other. For the peasantry are now split up into labourers and paupers, and for a long, long time now the King has not dared to exercise the least of the powers he has maintained only on paper.

Throughout the 18th century, right from the time of William of Orange, England, or rather Great Britain and Ireland, has been a monarchy in name only but a capitalist society in reality; and therefore if one seeks the Key to England's amazing prosperity in her constitution, one is definitely mistaken, which is so much more regrettable inasmuch as nearly everywhere in Europe people have believed since 1815 that if they could copy this always dangerous and by now completely antiquated and unacceptable constitution, they would have secured for themselves the lion's share in England's greatness and good fortune. However, I would not be expatiating on this matter, which may words cannot clarify anyway and which may even seem irrelevant to us, if it were not for the fact that I expect this building suddenly to collapse very soon, just as the old Houses of Parliament, which I managed to see both empty and in session, were burnt to the ground the other year and took the Stock Exchange with them.

You may smile, gentlemen, and ask whether I believe in omens. But I answer calmly: I don't believe in them, but I watch them, and when I have seen an institution heading for disaster for a long time, then I see in the collapse of its visible images and tools of power a sure sign of the Armageddon, which will annihilate it. This constitution, destroyed by the Stuarts in the middle of the 17th century and only badly stuck together again, has thus attracted my anxious attention for the best part of thirty years, and when I saw Canning[14] at the helm. I said to myself, 'If this building is to be saved, then he is the man to save it; time will show.' But when he fell from power in the first battle with capitalism, I declared rescue to be impossible, and time will soon show if I am right. If I am wrong, then it will not be the first time, and those who have never made a mistake can have a little laugh at me. But if the English constitution really is overthrown in our time, it is not my fault if my countrymen believe that it was freedom's final bulwark that crashed, whereas in fact it is only the main stronghold of capitalism, whose ramparts are being thrown up from the people's freehold land and whose moats are filled with the blood of the poor.

I have employed this imagery, gentlemen, because it is only through images that the intangible can be made visible; but you must not believe what is commonly said – that of necessity the truth is either half lost or completely lost through imagery. For the same who created the internal also created the external, and the latter to describe the former, so false representation in imagery and false representation in plain speaking have the same causes – on the one hand mendacity, on the other ignorance, so that imagery has simply come into disrepute because in an age of spiritual death people know neither how to employ it, nor how to appreciate it.

November 14th

Gentlemen,

... When one possesses some spiritual feeling oneself, it is impossible to see the holdness with which the Englishman attacks everything, the skill with which he immediately perceives what the success of the undertaking depends on, and the endurance with which he endeavours to overcome every difficulty – and usually does, – it is impossible to see all this without feeling that one is in the domain of a heroic genius, that genius to whom no thought is too high if Man can only reach it as one reaches the clouds from the highest mountain top, and to whom no great achievement is impossible before it is attempted with all the strength, diligence and tenacity which Man has in his power. And if we now enter the great workshops or watch the proud sailing-ships sweeping along on rivers and seas with the wind and the current, then we do not need to be able to copy all the ingenious appliances or work out the laws they follow in order to infer the existence of the spirit from its monumental works infer from the effects not only the wonderful powers that lie hidden in dumb nature but also those that lie closest to us: in the speaking, indeed eloquent, semidivine human nature – infer the hawk's eye that discovered what was hidden, and infer the knowledge that set the great powers of nature in motion to calculated effect, compelled the most untamable and terrible of all the powers of nature – as fire is – to slave and fight for Man to such an astonishing degree.

Well, gentlemen, among those who saw just some of the results you could hardly find a speaker eulogising English technology who knew less about what he was discussing and praising than I; and that would seem at first glance to make the eulogy not only suspicious but even ridiculous. But the opposite is really the case, because the results is a fact that no ignorance can minimize and no knowledge exaggerate; and if any evidence were required that every truth-loving thinker finds himself compelled to infer great effects from great causes, from the thousands of horse-power in the steam engine to human greatness and to the heroic genius of the North in the inventors, if proof was required of what only needs to be emphasised, then my praise would have the greatest validity, because it does not come at all naturally to me but is forced out of me on the self-evident truth itself. Well, gentlemen, I have been an enthusiast over many things, though not for as many as I have been blamed for. Where I go uncensored, you can be sure I never showed any excitement whatsoever, and that, is above all, true of mechanics and mathematics, about which I have not only said and written the most terrible things I knew, but also everything that I could think up. And you must not believe that the physicists' anathema have paralysed my tongue, or that their mathematical sermons have converted me into a worshipper of Demeter and Cybele longing to be initiated into their mysteries, or in plain Danish, that I now refer to dumb nature as the peasant did to his turkey-cock, 'If he doesn't talk he must be thinking even more'. No, I will not beguile you into superstition; I am proof against anathema, and the sermons, which I could not be bothered to listen to, did not move me an inch. So I say again as before I am sure that mechanics and mathematics can no more make any nation happy or any kingdom prosper than they have made or can make a soul blessed. I laughed just as loud at the University in Cambridge as I did here at home when I was assured that even for an able theologian mathematics was practically indispensable, and I laughed out loud in spite of the fact that in England they do not approve of talking loudly, except in church, nor of laughing loudly, except in Parliament.

The same thing could also happen to me tomorrow as happened the first time I went to the smithy at the Gammelholm Arsenal and saw the sledgehammer which worked on steam; it would still make me shiver, so that I would look around in fear to see where I really was: among living people or among trolls and black elves that made themselves invisible and perhaps before I knew it made the hammer dance on my head. Well, gentlemen, all that sort of thing, which looks like witchcraft and impresses itself with great force, contains for every poetic temperament something very sinister, so I must just gather my thoughts not to call it pure devilry, but rather admit that all the hammers are pieces of Mjollnir[16], which I love so much and which are the only real relics of the hammer of Thor that two thousand years ago split in pieces on the hard foreheads of the giants. Furthermore, gentlemen, the feeling does not have to be particularly poetic, but merely human, to fill us with a certain horror at machinery on a grand scale, which not only makes such a din that no one can hear himself speak, and blackens and fries everything that gets near to it, but also turns people in their thousands, both big and small, into accessories, mere appendices of the machinery, which is the main thing and basic force. So even those Englishmen who take the time to think about something other than making money watch in secret horror every new invention and application of mechanical forces on a colossal scale, which little by little will supersede all the old craftsmen and make them mere tools in the hand of the engineer, unthinking slaves in the manufacturer's works.

Therefore, if I dared to anathematize mathematics and outlaw machinery and condemn English industry as a monumental proof of a spiritual vacuum. I would do so willingly without asking whether it would help or not. But as I said, I dare not, I must not, I cannot, but on the contrary am compelled to admire the heroic genius which even in the desert can create a paradise, make even mathematics, in itself the deadest and emptiest of all our fields of knowledge, an incomparable stimulus to living industry in life and a lever for what is too difficult even for the united hands of giants. I really regret that the heroic spirit of Scandinavia does not do better, and in the language of spirit do far greater things than these. I regret that English industry is aiming more and more at what is called pure profit without caring about the means, and labours only for the present without a thought for the future. But I see more clearly every day that the reason for this lies no more in industry than it does in freedom, but in something quite different which would be still more grievous if one sat with one's hands in one's lap and performed no useful task whatsoever with eagerness and energy.

For as long as the national spirit is taking giant strides, it is undeniably on its legs, and as long as it performs what people cannot help but call great achievements, it is in its prime. And even if all the giant strides were false steps, and all the great achievements were dangerous ventures, life would still be far better than death, energy inestimably more useful than impotence. As long as there is life there is hope for the best that life can achieve, and as long as there is energy, a nation with a higher degree of enlightenment can correct its mistakes and prolong its days. So when I see what astonishing progress has been made in Russia by everything that can be driven by machines or managed by mechanical adaptation, I imagine that England will soon realize it is on the wrong road, sacrificing people in their hundreds of thousands to machinery and dissolving her spiritual energy in arithmetical sums and mathematical calculations; and then the same heroic genius, which has created the machines, will also realize that either they must be destroyed or they must be given a serviceable and serving relationship with man's industry and man's wellbeing. Just watch, gentlemen – you who are so much younger than I – and see how Russia, where the people are more primitive and a day's wages accordingly low will soon be able to supply the world market with an abundance of machine operators just as good, and a far better buy than the English, and see whether the Englishman, by exerting his spiritual energy finds new outlets for his industry in a direction where the Russian cannot, but we Norsemen can follow him, and given our poor means and modest ambition, I believe, without arousing the well-informed merman's wrath and envy. Call it a pipe dream if you like, for pipe dreams can be very worthwhile, even when they are not apparently fulfilled, if they help us to wake up cheerful, to rise healthy, and to do our best in good spirits.

Now, gentlemen, we are to approach the English spirit a little more closely, where it can appear more freely and reveal itself more clearly than through the machinery and the day-to-day pursuits that the English have in common with so many others, pursuits which have the daily breads as their primary aim, and unfortunately far too often in England wealth as their final aim. With this in mind we come first to the tunnel under the Thames and all that belongs to it; all those works of human hands whose only payment is the pleasure they offer, the great impression they give of the power the riches of the people and the glory with which the nation is thereby endowed.

I will forbear to give description either of the Thames tunnel or St. Paul's Cathedral or Westminster Abbey or England's capital in general, which is naturally the masterpiece of the national spirit in this field. Of course I have been struck by it like everybody else, but even the best descriptions of such things bore me, and how boring both for you and me must be such a bad description that would immediately show that I am just as great a dunce at architecture as at mathematics and engineering, and that is saying a lot. On the other hand I enjoy being surrounded by books and recalling the impression these things made on me, and you have led me to believe that at any rate it will not particary bore you.

The famous Thames tunnel or excavation half a mile from Customs House, begun in 1825 and according to the newspapers soon to be completed is without doubt a giant project and, what in England is an enormous incentive, so great a rarity that even in antiquity there is a legend of only one comparable structure, that is in Babylon under the Euphrates; and that was nothing compared to the English one, for Herodotus tells us that they diverted the river whilst they were building so they built only on the river bed, whereas here as far as possible they are building fourteen feet under the river-bed whilst the water is rising and falling, ships are sailing and anchoring above them as usual and it is undoubtedly tough, dangerous work, which will amaze everybody when it is finished. And people will not only be able to walk through the hole but will also drive in coaches, for it will measure 36 feet wide by 22 feet high. But the impression the masterpiece made on me was of the same kind as the descriptions of the wonders of Babylon and Egypt – the feeling of oppression, as if I was being buried alive.

I was indeed glad to emerge again and catch sight of St. Paul's Cathedral, which, whatever faults it may have, is nonetheless a magnificent work in the light of day above ground. This London wonder is in no way like the old gothic building of the same name which was completely destroyed in the great fire of 1666, but a work by England's famous freemason, Christopher Wren, who without ever having been to Italy designed it and watched over its execution for thirty-five years by the builder Thomas Strong with such success that St. Paul's now yields precious little to St. Peter's in Rome and St. Sophia's in Constantinople. The great architect himself lies buried here with an epitaph which states briefly: If you wish to see his monument, look about you. But that is easier said than done, for the great English churches I have seen were so divided up and closed in that I could never survey the whole, so the only thing that gave me an idea of the size of St. Paul's was a church festival I attended amid a large gathering of laity and clergy who were surrounded by about 20.000 children, I would imagine, arranged as if in an amphitheatre – and all this under the dome!

Westminster Abbey is the church with the royal tombs from the end of the 12th century and Poets' Corner, which is not really much, apart from Shakespeare and company, but nonetheless is more than any other nation has allowed its poets, for in Roskilde Cathedral there is not one of ours, not even Kingo.[17]

Westminster Hall, the remains of Edward the Confessor's castle and the St. Stephen's Chapel in the House of Commons: Here we stand again in Parliament, and here, where the subject is the expression of the national spirit I do not dare to brush it aside as I did when it was a question of the government. That two half governments in no way make a whole, but are on the contrary so imperfect that a whole is needed before anything can happen is a fact that I regard as being too obvious; but then nor was Parliament or the talking moot originally appointed to govern, but only to speak the heart's mind of the people as regards taxes as well as government in general. And I am convinced that such an institution belongs in every state which is to be properly organized. Now admittedly English society is neither well organized nor looks as if it soon will be, but that is partly because Parliament wishes to govern instead of just advising, and partly because of the peculiar lack of taste which is so typical of the English. Nevertheless, in the circumstances, Parliament has done England so significant a service that it is no wonder that all Englishmen find the history of their country really begins with Parliament, i.e. in the 13th century. We *must* remember that in the 11th century England was conquered by the Normans and as far as possible frenchified so that it was in the House of Commons that the mother tongue of the nation first manifested itself. Again, we must remember that in the golden days of classical Latin, in the 17th century, Latin completely superseded the mother tongue both in Germany and amongst us, something which would also have happened in England had not the House of Commons and the election speeches deriving from it sustained and revered it thereby keeping the national spirit alive, which always dies and rises again with the mother tongue.

This, gentlemen, is a profound historic truth which neither I nor anyone of our time can sufficiently impress upon all those who are willing to listen to us. For where the mother tongue in its natural simplicity is ousted from official usage and the cultured circles it is so to speak thrown on the dunghill. For it is there that it gradually loses, together with its refinement and its cultivation, all its higher forms of expression and thereby all its spiritual character and its power to move us; the learned and the cultured circles endeavour to assert a way of thought which is foreign to the people and cannot therefore be given living expression in the language of the people, and the people themselves cannot say what they think and feel. And since they cannot be transformed either, a lack of understanding and a tension arises between the Government and the subjects and between the learned and the unlearned which will increase day by day and inevitably lead to a violent revolution without it really helping very much.

This misfortune happens to some degree wherever church and school were latinized in the Middle Ages and only to a lesser degree since the Reformation, when the mother tongue was, indeed, introduced into the Church, but practically ousted therefrom again by being banned from the university where the clergy were being trained. And even in England, where Parliament put a stop to the speaking of Latin, the grammar school nevertheless daily corrupted what it could no supplant. So while the English ecclesiastical language is stone-dead, and Parliamentary language is half-dead, it is really only at the free public open-air meetings where the most radical members hold forth that the mother tongue is heard in its full vigour that is to say, only where revolution is being prepared and a bloodbath made ready.

November 16th

Gentlemen,

The English public spirit has been proverbial in Europe for so long that what I have attempted to demonstrate might seem entirely superfluous – namely the character and traces of this spirit both the evident and the concealed. But I fear that my attempt has been inadequate rather than superfluous; for usually people still have so superficial and so nebulous a conception of what spirit is that when one concedes to England the great advantage of having a spirit of her own, one seldom realizes fully what that involves, and even more seldom does one strive either to clarify for oneself what sort of spirit the English spirit is, or examine why the other civilized nations do not appear to possess any such spirit. Those who consider themselves best qualified in matters of public spirit and England's blessings therefore appear to think that it lies either in the air, or in the stout, or in the roast beef and potatoes, or that it descends like a *deus ex machina* from the machinery of the English constitution. And as far as I could see, the English are under the same delusion themselves, so since I am of a quite different opinion, it must seem rather more bold than superficial of me, with all the weapons I have to maintain my point of view. So bold I have to be, however, because if I am right, the welfare of the whole of Christendom and in particular of Scandinavia depends on England coming to an understanding of herself and on us coming to view England and her spirit in their proper light.

For if it is true that by 'public spirit' we are to understand neither more nor less than an invisible life-force which only to a greater or lesser degree is shared by all those who have a mother tongue in common, a life-force whose element is free activity and whose life-breath is the mother tongue, then that explains why nations became spiritless when they lost their freedom and as good as forgot their mother tongue, and shows which way they had to go if they wished to be rejuvenated in their old age and win the power to be themselves in their best moments – the highest goal a nation or an individual can reach here on earth. And if it is again true that the spirit or life-force in English industry is none other than the former well-known, world-renowed, unique, at present unappreciated or forgotten, heroic spirit of Scandinavia – if that is true, then there can be no more reasonable hope than this: that our Norse Spirit, parallel with the ascent of the mother tongue to her royal throne, will rise up on high here in Scandinavia, and England will acknowledge it as a prodigal son his venerable father. And what hope of great achievement should be too high in the near future, when England and our Scandinavia, reunited in spirit, like lobes of the common Danish tongue, combine their forces to honour the heroic genius of Scandinavia and show the world that his home was no land of barbarism where blood was drunk from enemy skulls, but a Valhalla where reconciliation was drunk in wine and mead with every noble adversary, and one fought merely to test one's strength and exercise oneself for the great contest for real gold and green woods in the golden-roofed Gimle[18] and the green home of the gods.

Well, gentlemen, the old imagery of Scandinavia came to life in me before I knew it, and that is the bardic vein in me, but it is also the source of my view and study of world history, as well as of my knowledge of history, if such lore I do, indeed, possess and shall acquire. And from this the boldness and the hope arose, with which, however desperate it may seem, I made it my endeavour that ancient imagery,[19] no longer heard from any lips, but only dimly scribbled on dark parchments in the smoke-stained Icelandic vellums, though dead and buried, manifest itself in the world of Midgard[20] anew, and do so at a time when all imagery was either despised or merely valued as a toy in the hands of the Roman usurper, who deliberately killed all gods that as a bastard son of Mars he might idolize himself on the throne of the world.

Thirty years ago, gentlemen, the situation really did look desperate for anyone who considered the matter with worldly wisdom. But thank goodness I was not among them, but was a daredevil in spirit who found it perfectly reasonable that a son of those people who crushed Rome in its imperial majesty and papal holiness could overcome the shadow of Rome in its classical purity, and that Norse imagery could and must become just as vital in all true Norsemen as it was in me. That is how it was then; but now that I have learned my lesson and know roughly how the world works and what the signs of the times are, now I say quite calmly: those clever heads of my youth made a false prediction. For although I was a trifle mad, nevertheless it was I who predicted correctly, because it was never more common at the close of the last century and the beginning of this that one heard the truth about spiritual matters out of the mouths of babes and sucklings, about which the clever heads were immensely stupid.

Now it may well seem, gentlemen, that it is still a bit early to pride oneself on the victory, since the Roman shadow, at least amongst us, still prides itself in its classical purity without all the lethal blows I gave it in my imagination appearing to have borne the least fruit; and similarly it seems as if Norse imagery is far closer to dying out in me than reviving in others. But appearances deceive: the battle is won and it is now only a question of how both I and the Nordic nations will exploit the victory. The shadow of Rome vanished in fact with the great Corsican and the supremacy of the French spirit of death in Europe. And I care as little for the treatment of Napoleon on St. Helena as I rejoice in spirit at the thought that this is what Latin and the French inanity can expect now that the Englishman, the natural Protector of Norse spirit, like Odin's son by Earth, the mighty, triumphant Thor, has regained the sceptre. For it is not just a dream that England's spirit, language, and literature, which from the middle of the past century began to fight against that of France both in Germany and in Scandinavia, but which seemed with the French Revolution and Napoleon's great feats to have lost everything, have made such surprising progress since the Battle of Waterloo that the decisive victory has been won. So it is just a question of whether I am right to regard the spirit of England and Scandinavia as one and the same. Because if that is so, Scandinavia must soon recognize its spirit in the English life and with spontaneous activity acquire it, and England must recognize its spirit in Norse imagery and with historical insight acquire that. Accordingly our line of action must be as far as our strength permits, along the Sound, at Gothenburg and Dover, and if not along the Thames then at least along the Humber. Well, gentlemen, that is the essence of my view of history, and a conviction that this basic relationship existed was the source of my joyful and firm hope now over thirty years old, and tottering only once because I wanted what was impossible: namely, to cleave shadows asunder and, inspire life with dead things. But the hope was reborn as soon as I realized the error of my ways.

A light really was lit for me, gentlemen, like a little sun which not only shone more brightly the higher it rose but also warmed my breast through and through with the gentle, calm and therefore also happy and lasting love of what is genuinely Danish and Scandinavian, above all as it is still found in our hearts and minds, however unappreciated and suppressed often by ourselves, however sick and pale, however faint and dying it may be. For when I realized that all writing is only a shadow and the outward sign of the living oral word, I saw not only how unreasonable all my indignation had been over the fact that neither old writing nor new could bring a rebirth of the Norse spirit and Denmark's heart, the Norse mentality and patriotic feeling amongst us. But I saw besides that just as surely as there is still a word in our mouth and heart which speaks for them and addresses all our kinsmen, just so surely will they have no need to be reborn, but only to be awakened, encouraged and strengthened by such a word. So it was only a matter of biding one's time, of patiently awaiting the moment when the word burst out of its own accord, as it is doing now, and found a response wherever I had kinsfolk – I who have neither created myself, my way of thinking or my language, but who think like our fathers and speak as my mother taught me. I am therefore now quite sure that as soon as we in Scandinavia just acquire as much spiritual freedom as they have in England – and I believe that we in Denmark are on the point of acquiring more – then in the course of a generation the heroic spirit of Scandinavia will make such strides as to astonish the world and such conquests that the peace-loving heart of Denmark will be overjoyed.

It is rather more doubtful, however, to what extent England will actively recall her Norse origins; for they seem forgotten, just as we have forgotten how we looked when we lay in the cradle. But if the hand of a master had painted us while we were lying there and our eye fell on the picture for a moment when childhood memories were visiting us, as they sometimes do, then I think we would clearly recognize it and be so fond of it that we would willingly buy it for a handsome sum. And that is what will happen to the Englishman when he discovers our Norse imagery which has not only attracted him of old as much as the rest of us but so obviously originated in his mind and agrees with his history.

To make it clear, however, I must put the question historically and ask whether the Englishman will acknowledge his father, the Anglo-Saxon, and honour his memory. For as soon as he does so, we have got him at once, not just because, the Venerable Bede says that the Anglo-Saxon came from here, but because the Englishman must be able to see it at once in Anglo-Saxon poetry, of which fortunately there are great monuments. Now it was precisely for the sake of these memorials that our dear King with his paternal heart for our national heritage allowed me to journey to England in the years 1829-1831 when I could do nothing here at home. And nobody knows better than I how the Englishman regards the Anglo-Saxon, for I represented him in London, in Oxford and Cambridge, even indeed in Exeter and Bristol, that is, as far as his old boundary with Cornwall and Wales. The prime object of the journey was to examine the Anglo-Saxon manuscripts in the British Museum and wherever else they might be, and in a decent way as far as possible to steal the best, that is, I made a little Viking raid, as best I could in this day and age. But of course it required more than that to drive an old stay-at-home like me over the North Sea at my time of life when I had grown so attached to my children and books and daily routine. Yes indeed, it required much more than that to make me, who until that day never spoke anything but Danish if I could help it, endeavour to acquaint myself with a foreign language. So to this end the hope of conquering England was required, or at least of preparing the only great conquest that the Danish people from days of old had the desire and good fortune to make.

Thus my main aim was to get into contact with the Englishman and win him for the Anglo-Saxon and so for Scandinavia.

Notes

1. Merlin de Thionville (1762-1832) Grundtvig refers to him as a Jacobin, though he was in opposition to that faction and belonged to the group that brought down Robespierre.
2. Æsir or Asir were the Scandinavian heathen gods.
3. The Fenris Wolf was a monster, a son of Loki, the evil trickster god, which is fettered by the gods, but whose escape signals the coming of Ragnarok, the twilight of the gods.
4. Grundtvig alludes to Napoleon whom Grundtvig regarded as a great peril to Christianity and European culture as he expresses it in a pamphlet "A strange Prediction – also about Denmark" (1814).
5. Adam Gottlob Oehlenschlaeger (1779-1850) is the leading poet of Danish Romanticism. Grundtvig was enthralled by his early work, but came to regard his interpretation of the Nordic heroic past as shallow and misleading.
6. 1815-1820 was a period of political unrest in Germany particularly centred in German universities and harshly put down by the authorities.
7. Karl August Hardenberg (1750-1820) was Chancellor of Prussia from 1810 and, though responsible for measures against the liberals, also active for liberal reform in various fields.
8. Dannevirke is the ancient Danish system of fortifications in Schleswig protecting against invaders from the south. It dates from the 9th century or earlier.
9. Joseph Görres (1776-1848) is a romantic writer who began his career as a radical enthusiast for the French Revolution. In his later years he moved to an extreme conservative position in politics and religion.
10. Polignac (1780-1847). Ultramontanist Prime Minister of France under Charles X immediately prior to the Revolution of 1830.
11. Gert is a character in Ludvig Holberg's comedy "Gert the Westphalian". This loquacious barber bores his customers beyond endurance with his account of a journey he once made from Haderslev to Kiel in Schleswig-Holstein.
12. Secondary schools with a modern languages and science curriculum were introduced in Denmark in 1837 and regarded by Grundtvig with extreme distrust. See p. 65.
13.
14. Grundtvig refers to "the Assizes of Jerusalem" instituted by Godfrey of Bouillon in 1099.
15. George Canning (1770-1827). British Foreign Secretary and Prime Minister.

16. Mjollnir is the hammer of the Norse God Thor and the seat of his formidable strength.
17. Thomas Kingo (1634-1703) is Denmark's greatest Baroque poet and hymnist.
18. At Gimle is the gold-thatched hall where the Gods will dwell after Ragnarok, and where they will recover their golden tables pieces among the grass of the evergreen plains.
19. By imagery Grundtvig understands the Norse myths which he regarded as symbolic expressions of the heroic spirit of Scandinavia, and which, when properly interpreted, might serve as an inspiration for life in the modern age.
20. Midgard is in Norse cosmology the human world.

VI

Selections from Elementary Christian Teachings

Elementary Christian Teachings first appeared as individual essays in a periodical for Christian knowledge, *Kirkelig Samler*, edited by Christian M. Kragballe, 1855-1861. They were published together as a book of 21 chapters in 1868.

It is no textbook of orthodoxy, nor is it a primer for school-children. Grundtvig makes it clear that he has written not so much a new book on dogmatics as one of antidogmatics. Grundtvig wants to assist Christians in recovering the simple faith of childhood. His book is consequently an attempt to demonstrate what immediate faith is, unconfounded by orthodoxy and rationalism.

In a manner characteristic of Grundtvig he presupposes the existence of a tangible substance "For other foundation can no man lay than that which is laid, which is Jesus Christ" present in persons "We must inquire of the Church what sort of a foundation it is that the Apostles have laid in the name of Christ." Faith has its starting-point in an existing fellowship of flesh and blood. The body of faith is no abstract entity, neither an ideology nor a fraternity, but a gathering of people with one thing in common, that they are ready to accept the testimony of the Holy Spirit. The Church of flesh and blood existing in time and space is a historical fact as the Church of God forgathered around baptism and communion for two thousand years. This objective historical truth is the objective correlative of the subjectivity of faith. In this way Grundtvig strikes a subtle balance between subjective arbitrariness and objective dogmatics.

Elementary Christian Teachings place Grundtvig's view of Christianity at the centre of the theological debate of his day. The distinction between true Christianity in an academic sense and the truth of Christianity, meaning the existential validity of Christianity to the individual, had been analysed with logical stringency by Kierkegaard in "The Philosophical Fragments" (1844), and in "The Instant" (1855) Kierkegaard put forward the polemical view that the Christianity of the New Testament did not exist. Elementary Christian Teachings may be regarded as Grundtvig's alternative to this literal-minded Christianity. It is no polemical counter to Kierkegaard's critique, but a complete repudiation. The fact that man was created by his Maker and in advance placed in a relationship Grundtvig considered a sufficient argument against Kierkegaard's incisive analysis. While Kierkegaard is the out-and-out intellectualist, Grundtvig places faith where it properly belongs: in the community of the Church. The criteria of Christianity are not, as with Kierkegaard, the intensity of reflection but "the Christian signs of life". Against intellectualism Grundtvig points to the vitality of faith, its steadfastness and immediate manifestations. Faith must be embodied.

What mattered to Grundtvig was not faith versus knowledge but conviction versus doctrinalism. That was what he had to offer those of his century who struggled to add experience to a theology that threatened to ratiocinate the existential content out of Christianity. His aim in this respect coincided with Kierkegaard's, but whereas Kierkegaard will give meaning to Christianity in terms of reflection, Grundtvig wants to subordinate reflection to the terms of immediate faith. Elementary Christian Teachings do not intend to teach Christians anything new about Christianity, but wish to rehabilitate the conviction they have forgotten because of too much reflection and doctrinalism.

In this way Elementary Christian Teachings link up with Grundtvig's view of man and his philosophy of culture. It is the theological part of a general show-down with all cultural paternalism. Man of flesh and blood, i.e. imperfect man, is the starting-point of all Grundtvig's ideas about culture for the people. Grundtvig is an anti-idealist, because he rejects all ideology condemning sinful man. Elementary Christian Teachings present Grundtvig as a common-sense theologian: the preaching of Christianity is not instruction about culture but engagement in it. The preaching of Christianity ought not to be a foreign body in secular culture. If it attaches itself to the people's experience of life and is combined with a varied programme for the education of the people it may provide an elitist culture with a closeness to life in which it tends to be lacking.

Hellmut Toftdahl

Elementary Christian Teachings[1]

When those of us who together with Martin Luther have parted
company with the Pope in Rome and got rid of everything we consider to be popery, when we hear talk of the elementary Christian
teachings, we consider them to be either what the clergy whom we
regard as Christian teach our children or demand that they learn for
the public examination which takes place here before they are admitted to Holy Communion; either that, or we consider them to be
the five sections of Martin Luther's Primer which we call his little
catechism. In the first case, our ideas of the elementary Christian
teachings are vague and uncertain, and in the second case we take
it for granted that 'Lutheran' means in all respects the same as
'Christian', and that one can be brought up to be a Christian by
reading a book and learning it by heart. But neither of these assumptions holds true, since it goes without saying that the elementary
Christian teachings must include all the essentials of Christianity
that Our Lord Jesus Christs Himself and the apostles who had his
unlimited authority have laid down as the basis of the Church, as
the apostle Paul writes: 'For other foundation can no man lay than
that which is laid, which is Jesus Christ'.

We must not therefore blindly assume that what Martin Luther
or some other teacher in the Church many hundreds of years after
the Apostles calls the elementary Christian teachings really are
that, but must inquire of the Church what sort of a foundation it is
that the Apostles have laid in the name of Christ, and have laid not
in a book but in the Church itself as a community of Christian
people.

On the other hand, what we *must* so to speak blindly assume is
that Christ has a Church on earth and that we can find it; but we
already assume this in the very fact that we ask the question, what
are the elements of Christianity you teach to children? For where
there are no parents there are no children either, so that if there
were no more Christian parents on earth, there would be no more

Christian children; and if there were no Christian Church on earth, there would be no Christian people, young or old, and no elementary human teachings for the children that could justifiably be called Christian. So when we seriously ask about the elementary Christian teachings, it must be assumed either that we ourselves are already members of Christ's community, or that we are thinking of becoming so, when we have learnt what the essentials of Christianity are and can make up our mind to accept them. I therefore assume here that the so-called Lutheran Church, into which I was admitted through baptism, was and is a part of Christ's Church, which the Apostles established according to Christ's own institution and in His name, and which will last until the end of the world; so that far from establishing a brand-new Church, Martin Luther was both before and after he parted company with the Pope in Rome, a member of and a faithful servant in the Church of our Lord Jesus Christ.

Now in this Church of Christ we must all know that baptism in the name of the Father, the Son and the Holy Ghost is the only way of gaining admission, with the witness that this baptism takes place not only with water but with 'water and spirit' and is therefore not merely a so-called Church practice (a ceremony) but a heavenly rebirth in water, through which the Holy Ghost in the name of Our Lord Jesus Christ grants forgiveness of sins and the child's right to a Father in heaven together with the hope of eternal life.

This is said and witnessed explicitly at every baptism into Christ's Church, of which Martin Luther was a member and teacher and of which I am a member and teacher, so this is undeniably a major part of this Church's witness concerning the elementary Christian teachings, for the essentials of Christianity undeniably include both in which way and by what means one becomes a Christian, and what a person gains and inherently turns into by becoming a Christian – by really being admitted into Christ's Church.

But just as baptism with water in the name of the Father, the Son and the Holy Ghost now teaches us in which way and by what means a person is admitted into Christ's Church and becomes a Christian; and just as the Lord's blessing at baptism – 'Peace be with you' – teaches us that becoming a Christian brings peace with God and the forgiveness of sins; and just as the Lord's Prayer, which through baptism is placed in the mouth of the whole of Christ's Church and at baptism in the mouth of each individual

Christian, teaches us that by becoming a Christian a person becomes a child of God; so does the baptismal covenant teach us what kind of Father, and what kind of Son, and what kind of Holy Ghost it is in whose name a person is baptized a Christian, and teaches us in full what is demanded of each person who through the baptism instituted by the Lord wishes to be admitted into Christ's Church. This means the renunciation of the Devil and all his deeds and all his nature; and belief in God the Father, who is the one true God, the Maker of heaven and earth; and in Jesus Christ, His only begotten Son, who is the Son of Man, Jesus Christ; and in the Holy Ghost, through whom the Virgin Mary conveived and bore Jesus, and who is the divine soul in the whole of Christ's Church; and in the Fellowship of the Saints around our Lord Jesus Christ, and belief in Him concerning the forgiveness of sins, the resurrection of the flesh and the everlasting life, just as the Apostles' Creed pronounces it at baptism.

This vocal and clear witness of the congregation at baptism to the baptism itself, to its conditions and its fruits, this witness of Christ's Church, which must be accepted and believed in as His Apostles' and His own witness, passed on from mouth to mouth and generation to generation as the Word from His own mouth which must never vanish from the mouths of His congregation and from which His Spirit will never vanish but must always accompany and seal the witness, *these*, in the truest, strictest and most blessed sense, are the elementary Christian teachings, which not only can and will enlighten all who have ears to hear of the rebirth to God's children through belief in the gospel of Christ, but which at the same time can and must revive the spiritually half-dead. So the elementary Christian teachings contain and announce the saving power of Christ's gospel in the Holy Ghost to every human heart that believes the witness of the Lord and His Church.

This witness and these elementary Christian teachings also correspond wonderfully well with what the Scriptures call Christ's teaching, through which He Himself becomes the teacher of the whole Church, and with what the Scriptures call God's witness concerning His only begotten Son and the eternal life in Him that imparts eternal life to all those who in faith take up the witness, the eternal life, and what the Scriptures point to as the Word of Faith. This Word of Faith must be the heart and soul of all our Christian preaching, and must bring the Church so close to Christ as the

Word in its mouth and in its heart that it never asks who will go up to heaven to bring Christ down or down to hell to bring Him up from the dead, but with the confession of this Word in its mouth and with the belief in this Word in its heart feels sure of salvation.

If with this Christian enlightenment we now turn from the Church to Luther's little catechism as the book which has long borne the name of the Elementary Christian Teachings, then I believe we shall find that of all the books we have read there is none that has a greater claim to bearing that name, to the extent that any book *can* bear it, because it reminds us throughout of the elementary Christian teaching that we have found in the baptism of Christ's Church. But we see in addition that Luther's catechism can no more than any other book by an individual Christian scribe, or even by an Apostle, bear remote comparison with the witness and the elementary teachings in the mouth of the whole Church with a living voice.

I find it hard now to go into further detail about this, partly because Luther's catechism really does mark a giant step forward in Christian education and for over three centuries has contributed more than any other book to fixing the attention on faith and baptism, and partly because this little book has been very dear to my heart both since my childhood days and from the first years of my ministry. But since this book is now being invoked against the voice of the Church and the Lord, it is necessary to point out that even as a statement of the elementary Christian teachings, which anyway could never take the place of the living and only valid witness of the Church, even as such a statement this little book contains great mistakes and shortcomings, inasmuch as it contains both too much and too little, and describes only fragments of the elementary Christian teachings, without pointing to their Christian consequences and contexts; and finally it confuses the witness of the Church with the individual's opinion on it and explanation of it.

As a statement of the elementary Christian teachings there is too much in Luther's catechism, for as Luther himself has realized, illustrated and urgently impressed upon us, the first part with the ten commandments does not belong to the elementary Christian teachings, and this alone is what is under discussion. So it is quite another matter whether Christian parents do good or ill, or act wisely or unwisely in impressing the ten commandments of Moses upon their pupils for the illumination of the divine law, which Christ's gospel has in no way come to repeal but rather to confirm and, with the removal of the law's curse, to fulfil through love.

What is peculiar to Christ and His gospel and what constitutes the essence of Christianity, that, which in its entirety and excluding all else must constitute the elementary Christian teachings, is one thing: what and how much Christ's gospel presupposes in the children of Man who of necessity must be both willing and able to believe the gospel and to be blessed by God's grace, is quite another thing. For precisely because the gospel, as the offer of God's love, presupposes the law, as the command of God's love, precisely for this reason the gospel itself is not a law and cannot contain either a little or a lot of the law within it.

But just as Luther's catechism, when it is regarded as a description of the elementary Christian teachings, contains too much by including the commandments of the Mosaic law, so does it include too little by omitting the renunciation of the Devil and all his deeds and all his nature, which obviously belongs to the essentials of Christianity, since it is an inseparable part of the baptismal covenant in the Christian Church, and only thus does the Christian baptismal covenant in spirit and truth become valid as the sole condition of entry into the Kingdom of God.

Finally, the faith of the Christian Church, the Lord's Prayer and the Lord's own institutions – baptism and Holy Communion – are described in Luther's catechism only out of their Christian context, as if in this way they each had their own separate authority and importance, in spite of the fact that it is clear that the so-called 'Three Articles of Faith' only acquire their proper authority and importance as inseparable parts of the unshakable creed of the Christian Church at baptism, and that this creed only has validity as a condition of baptism when it is combined with the renunciation. It is equally clear that the 'Lord's Prayer' is only an expression and a confirmation of the hope of the whole Church, being the hope of God's children, because at the baptism instituted by the Lord it is put into the mouth of the whole Church, and baptism is a bathing of rebirth and renewal only when it is in an indissoluble union with the baptismal covenant, just as ultimately Holy Communion is only fellowship with Christ's body and blood on the condition of faith and baptism.

What follows from this is as clear as daylight, namely, that insofar as a book has any right whatsoever to carry the title of Elementary Christian Teachings for children then a much better book on the teaching of children is needed than Martin Luther's as a description of the Lord's own institutions, that is, Holy Baptism and Holy Communion including everything that in origin and nature belongs to them and nothing more besides, partly because the Lord's own institutions must be assumed to contain all that belongs to becoming a child of God and the birthright to inheriting eternal life, and partly because the Lord's own institutions are the only ones that can be traced back clearly and with certainty to the Lord, without whom we can do nothing at all. Thus they can be distinguished from all the words and deeds of all other individuals, and distinguish His Spirit from all other spirits.

Such a description of the elementary Christian teachings, which also drew attention to the fact that the words of communion do not belong to the elementary Christian teachings strictly speaking, but are only the explanation of the elementary teachings for adults, offering them the first fruits of God's Kingdom; such a book might nowadays be considered indispensable, and can obviously be of much use when properly used. But it can obviously do just as much damage by being misused, and although it would have much in common with all visible or invisible life and light, with everything that truly enlivens and enlightens and therefore first and last with Christ's gospel, nevertheless, when writing and recommending such a book we ought to take great pains to ensure that its correct use can be so distinguishable from its misuse that as far as possible all unwitting misuse is thereby avoided.

To this end it will be far from sufficient to ensure solemnly that we do not put such a book either in place of, or alongside the united, vocal and living witness of the Lord and His Church at baptism and communion, but must also show as clearly as possible that all the reflection of Christian life and light that such a book may have is borrowed from the real life and light of the Lord's own institutions, so that the description borrows its reflection of divine life from the life of God's children which the Lord creates with His vocal Divine Word and grants in the bathing of rebirth and renewal and further nourishes and strengthens with His vocal Divine Word, fosters and satisfies in the fellowship of His body and blood. And it borrows its reflection of Christian enlightenment from the light of life which the Lord Himself has lit and has not hid under a bushel but has set in the words of the baptismal covenant in a candleholder to shine for all those who are in the house. Furthermore it is to them we must show as clearly as possible through the whole life of the Church right from the Apostles' days on earth down to our own, that whenever the proper relationship between 'the voice of the Lord' and its description has been forgotten by the Church, then the so-called orthodoxy, however biblical it may have been, was nevertheless only appearance without power, which could neither extend, defend, nor prove itself, and indeed did not even realize that true Christianity can and must do these things, and can be neither extended, defended nor proved by worldly means, be they worldly power, worldly wisdom or worldly pleasure.

If one now says what many both have said and will say, namely, that this Christianity is not "the Christianity of the New Testament", then in a way one has appearances on one's side. For if by the 'New Testament' one understands only the book to which the name of the 'New Testament' has been given and not the New Covenant itself, which is the baptismal covenant, then indeed we ourselves confess that our Christianity is not some sort of book Christianity, but the Christianity of Christ and His Church. But in our mouth that is only the same as saying that our Christianity is not a dead but a living Christianity, not a shadow but a reality. And those who demand 'New Testament Christianity' will presumably not admit that they do not mean anything living, real or active by it but only a lifeless reflection and a powerless shadow.

On the other hand, if one is of the opinion that the Christianity which we derive from and base on Christ and the united, vocal and living witness of His Church at baptism and communion as instituted by Our Lord Jesus Christ, that this Christianity should not be in agreement with the Apostolic writings that are called the 'New Testament', then one will doubtless carry the burden of proof until the Day of Judgement. For we boldly dare to claim that our Christianity not only harmonizes with the whole of that part of the so-called 'New Testament' that either itself purports to be Apostolic writings or can with some grounds be presented as such, but that it is also the only Christianity that *does* harmonize with it.

For the Apostolic writings no more call themselves the 'New Testament' than they purport at any point to be the doctrinal foundation of Christianity, or the rule of Faith, the voice of the Lord, the source of life or the body of Christ. So that if one tries to present them as being a little or a large part of everything which, according

135

to the Apostolic writings, must be found in true Christianity, then this will be done in open contradiction of the Apostolic writings, which throughout refer to a vocal, living, almighty Word of God to all of us, a Word which is both 'Spirit and Life' – that is, the Heavenly Father's own Spirit and Our Lord Jesus Christ's own life – so that no Christianity that lacks that Spirit and that life can in any way harmonize with the Apostolic writings.

Now just as Christianity according to the Apostolic writings must really be a power of God to salvation, so must this power of God, according to the same writings, reveal and prove itself in its effect on all the believers and the baptized that make up Christ's people and Church on earth, so that this Church, treading in the footsteps of the 'Son of Man', achieves a divine growth from Christian childhood to Christian manhood, in fact measuring up to the Lord Himself, not as His rival but as His bride and partner in marriage. And yet it will be found that all those who wish to lay another sort of Christian foundation than that which is laid in and at baptism as instituted by the Lord, that they either do not wish to know anything at all about a new human life in the Lord's Spirit that is characteristic for the Christian Church, regarding it as sheer mystical nonsense and fantastical illusion, or they show quite clearly that they know nothing at all about it, inasmuch as they pass something off as spiritual life and Christian growth and perfection that neither resembles the Lord's life on earth nor can harmonize with the Apostolic writings.

Finally it is clear that according to the Apostolic writings not only must the true Christianity as the revelation of the Heavenly Father's love be incomparably the most attractive to all 'the little ones' in every sense: the children under age, the simple-minded and the humble, but furthermore experience must prove that the true Church consists principally of those who have no standing in this world as regards high birth, wealth and power or scholarship and knowledge. So it is clearly impossible that such a form of Christianity, which is derived from and based on books – and in particular on an old book whose origin is obscure, whose authenticity can be doubted at any moment, whose original languages can only be very few and even those imperfectly known, and whose correct interpretation must be a bone of contention between believers and disbelievers and genuine and false scholars till kingdom come – that such a form of Christianity should harmonize with the Apostolic writings; nor is it possible that a Church in which the secular scholars and intellectuals were the heart and soul could, according to the Apostolic writings, be apostolic.

Of course, without apparently contradicting oneself one can claim that our Christianity, which we derive from and base on Christ and His Church united in the vocal and living witness in and at baptism and communion as instituted by the Lord, that this does not tally with the Apostolic account either; nor that it contains the spirit and the life within it that the Apostolic writings presuppose and which *must* be found in that Christian gospel which is to be a power of God for salvation to all believers. But nonetheless, since this is apparently the only sort of Christianity that can possibly correspond to the Apostolic account, in defending it we have two great advantages over all our opponents: firstly, that we can point to the future as the settler of the dispute, and secondly that we can show that Christianity stands or falls with Our Lord Jesus Christ in heaven and His Church on earth.

As regards the first, it is obvious that only the future can clearly show whether our Christianity corresponds to the Apostolic account or not, for whether or not our Christianity is a power of God for salvation can only be seen from its effect on people after it has begun to operate, that is, after a Church great or small has freely acquired this Christianity shown in baptism and communion and has won a position in which it is recognizable from every other so-called Christian Church. For as long as we are lumped together with a whole mass of people who for worldly reasons apparently have the creed, baptism and communion in common with us, then the effect of God's power, which can only work on a minority, will of necessity be thrown into the shade, where it can easily be overlooked. Furthermore, it is self-evident according to both the Apostolic writings and the laws of human life that the life of the Church only reaches its goal at the end of the course; so that during its growth it cannot be fully-grown, nor therefore can it completely live up to the account which the Spirit has given for the present of what He who searches all hearts knows in advance.

As for the second point, that our Christianity, which we derive from and base on Christ and His Church's united, vocal and living witness in and through baptism and communion as instituted by the Lord Himself, stands or falls with Christ and His Church, this is also self-evident, since one cannot point to any Church with a different baptism and a different communion that can possibly be based on Christ's own institution. So that if ours was not so either, then Christ would have no Church now, and would not have had for many centuries on earth, and could not be God's only-begotten Son with all power in heaven and on earth, and would not have been and could not be together with His Church always even unto the end of the world.

We can smile at all the possible objections to the validity of this Christianity, which we derive from and base on Christ and His Church's united, vocal and living witness in and at baptism and communion as instituted by Our Lord Jesus Christ, and we shall see them blown away like chaff before the wind if we only stand firm in our faith in Jesus Christ and the Holy Spirit, which is the Spirit both of the Father and of the Son, both of love and of truth, the divine governor in God's kingdom, so long as it only exists in spirit. But we must admit that according to the Apostolic writings and all Christian experience this faith is always besieged by doubt and exposed to danger here on earth, since being in God's eyes far more precious than gold it must also undergo an ordeal by fire. Yet it is a great consolation that where a child's faith, such as it is amongst us, far from having to bear the weight of the elementary Christian teachings, is actually borne up *by* it, as the Lord's own teaching, there the tempter of innocent faith immediately has to face up to Him who has proved that he is the 'seed of woman' that breaks the serpent's head and will always show He is the good shepherd from whose hand no wolf can tear the lamb.

For these elementary teachings of our Lord are the 'shield of faith' by which we can extinguish all the Devil's flaming arrows, and since our course between baptism and communion is precisely the living road between faith and love, so our Christian hope grows with every step as the hope of glory in God's children. And through its wonderful strength in battle against all fear it will become clear to us as 'Christ within us', in whom we are equal to everything precisely when we believe and feel that without Him we can do nothing at all.

Notes

1. Elementary Christian Teachings chapter I, first published in 1855.
2. I Cor., iii, 11.

Concerning our Third Article of Faith

The true, original Christianity is a new thing on earth, something that nobody knows unless he has heard God's Word about it and believes the Word, as it is written: How should they call upon the Lord without believing in Him, and how should they believe without having heard? For faith comes from hearing God's Word. That is why the Apostles of our Lord Jesus Christ wrote their Christian instructions only for Christians and to Christians who had heard and believed and were baptised with Christian baptism. Bishops and priests of later times, who should be the Apostles' successors, have only seldom taken note of this and followed it. And this is a major reason for the confusion we have created for ourselves concerning the proper meaning of the Apostles' writings and all other Christian questions which to no avail, and in fact to our great cost, we have preferred to quarrel and haggle with the unbelieving Bible-readers about rather than throw light on them for the believing Christians. So that when we wish to enlighten and benefit the Church with our Christian writings, we must return to the Apostolic practice, keep the believers in mind, and address our writings to them alone, with the express addition that we are well aware that the unbelieving, should the writings come to their notice, cannot understand our attitude at all, and in fact can only misunderstand it.

What I am therefore writing here about our "Third Article of Faith" I am writing only to those and for those who both know how it is read at baptism and also believe in its content. So that when I nevertheless allow this essay to appear in print, it is only because this is the best means by which it can come to the notice of Danish-speaking believers and because the whole world is welcome to see what I, as a believing Christian and servant of the Word, write to my fellow-Christians about the common faith.

So I beg you all first to notice especially that what we are used to calling, according to Martin Luther's little children's book[1], 'The Three Articles of Faith', is only a division into three of that

'Word of Faith' which is always heard at Christian baptism and on the basis of which baptism takes place when that 'Word of Faith' is fully confessed with a vocal 'yes' to the questions concerning it.

Next I beg you to lay it to heart that this Word of Faith at baptism which from time immemorial has been commonly known as 'the Apostles' Creed' is the one half of our baptismal covenant; that is, the agreement which we make on Our Lord's behalf with all those who at the baptism instituted by the Lord and in the name of the Father and of the Son and of the Holy Spirit wish to become members of the Church of Our Lord Jesus Christ and thereby have a share in the forgiveness of sin and in the sure hope of salvation which He has promised to grant to all those who 'believe' and are 'baptized'. So it is self-evident that whoever either only pretends to answer yes to this covenant and agreement, or afterwards goes back on his word, derives no benefit whatsoever from his baptism and gains no part or share at all in what the Lord has promised only to those who truly believe His word and remain faithful unto death.

Finally, I assume here that you are reasonably well acquainted with this creed with regard to what it tells us about God the Father, our Creator, and about God's Son, our Lord Jesus Christ, our Redeemer, but that most of you are in great need of further enlightenment concerning the Holy Spirit and the part in the creed at baptism which expresses its work for our salvation.

For I have noticed over the years now that many of you who understood quite clearly what we confess at baptism concerning 'the Father and the Son' were in considerable doubt as to what it actually is that we then confess concerning the Holy Spirit; and since the reason for this may, indeed must, lie to a great extent in the obscurity of these words through which the so-called Third Article of Faith is translated into our mother tongue, and in the inadmissable alterations to the words which have been made at will and which it has been attempted to introduce into Our Lord's unchangeable baptism. So I will now endeavour to shed light on both points for my fellow-believers.

We Christian scribes who have learnt how the Creed is worded in Greek and Latin from those from whom we have received our baptism and our Christianity, and we who are better enlightened about the Christian order or Salvation from the writings of the Apostles in original Greek – we all know that just as our First Article of Faith gives expression to the reason why God has looked after us so lovingly and will forgive us, even though we have all sinned, precisely because He is the 'Father' from whom all fatherliness receives its name both in heaven and on earth, and because He is our Creator, who would not have created all people in His likeness to no purpose, so does our Second Article of Faith give expression to the manner in which God reveals His gracious, fatherly regard for us by giving us His only begotten Son, who is the judge of all the living and the dead, as Saviour and Redeemer. Finally, our Third Article of Faith gives expression not only to the fruits of God's mercy to us and of the incarnation of His only begotten Son, but also to the means by which God's mercy in Christ is granted and bears the fruits of salvation amongst us; that is to say that the Spirit of God the Father and of Our Lord Jesus Christ, the Spirit of Grace and Truth, with God's spoken word summons us to Holy Baptism, where we who believe the Word receive forgiveness of sins, are reborn to the everlasting life and summons again the believers and baptized to Holy Communion, where all worthy communicants, by participating in the Lord's own body and blood, receive through their love of God and their neighbour a living fellowship in body and soul around everlasting life.

Thus the baptismal creed is a rich essence not of any writings but of God's evangelical counsel for our salvation, the Word of Faith which the Lord Himself has laid on the lips of the Apostles and all His Church, in order thereby both to separate clearly His people and His kingdom from all the peoples and kingdoms of this world, and to give all His Church a Word of God on which it can safely build its faith and through which it can distinguish His Spirit from all the spirits of the world and the spirits of delusion. But early on this fundamental Christian enlightenment was obscured particularly by the fact that contrary to the Lord's strict injunction those who should have been Christ's servants and ministers of the Church after the Apostles set themselves up as rulers of the Church and its faith, as if some of them were what the Spirit of the Lord alone is, namely, the all-powerful Governor in the kingdom of our ascended King on earth – or at least as if it was only bishops and priests and not the whole Church of believers and baptized that Our Lord Jesus Christ can and wants to enlighten, strengthen, govern and sanctify with His Father's Spirit.

This fundamental error of the papists was already discovered by Martin Luther, who rightly lashed this self-glorification by which the Roman Pope and his so-called lords spiritual (in German: 'geistlichkeit') replaced the Holy Spirit with themselves, or had at least fooled people into believing that they alone had the Holy Spirit and were themselves men of the spirit whom all the rest of the Church should blindly believe and follow in the matter of salvation. But even though Luther's action was a giant step towards separating our three Articles of Faith in our baptismal covenant from all the self-made articles in excess of them, and a giant step towards grasping and understanding our Third Article of Faith correctly by following the Spirit which alone calls, gathers, enlightens and sanctifies the whole Church and which has begun its good deed and will accomplish it before the Day of Our Lord Jesus Christ; nevertheless, it was still not enough. For the scribes somehow replaced the Pope and his clergy by claiming that our three Articles of Faith were extracted from the Bible, which they alone knew how to interpret correctly. In this way the scribes elevated themselves when they actually admitted that the whole believing and baptized Church had the Holy Spirit, but nonetheless claimed that only the few who had scrutinized the Scriptures could be enlightened on the question of faith and salvation.

Anyway, even if our scribes had kept strictly to the Creed at baptism and given it a unanimous witness, it would nevertheless, through their assertion of the necessity of biblical scholarship for a sure faith and salvation, have been their own fault when the Church sank as deeply into confusion as it sank previously into superstition, and was then in doubt especially as to who had the Holy Spirit and what the whole Church could expect of it.

But in addition the scribes made the Third Article of Faith, which in our mother tongue was already very unclear, even more obscure by acting completely on their own account and substituting and saying 'Christian Church' for 'catholic Church', 'the Resurrection of the Body' for 'the Resurrection of the Flesh' and finally by interpolating the addition of their own making 'after death' between 'Resurrection' and 'the Everlasting Life'.

I say that our Third Article of Faith was already much more obscure in our language than it needed or ought to have been because we used the foreign or made-up word 'kirk' insted of 'congregation' or 'assembly' (in Greek and Latin: ekklesia) and the vague word 'community' instead of 'fellowship'. But matters got much worse when they substituted the word 'Christian', which scholars will quarrel over until Judgement Day, for the word 'catholic', which everyone could see was meant to express what was the same always and everywhere; and when by putting the resurrection of the 'body' instead of the 'flesh' they tempted the Church to dream of another sort of body from that of 'flesh and bones' with which Our Lord rose from the dead; and when they actually interpolated the home-made 'after death', which inevitably caused the Church to think that it was not until *after* death that Our Lord would give us a share in the everlasting life, even though He has promised all His believers to open with His Spirit a well-spring of life within them that flows with the promise of eternal life.

I would like to tell the Church what excuses can be made among men for both the old and the new errors, whose intention was certainly not to distort the Creed, but partly it would be too long-winded and even unclear for the majority of readers, and partly I must ask the Church first and last to take note that Our Lord cannot possibly regard any excuse by His servants as valid when they distort His Word, whether convincingly or not, as the consequences are always the same for the Church, which, when it fails to take God's Word pure and simple, cannot understand it properly either or enjoy its full blessing.

Thus as Christian scribes it must be our chief care to enlighten the Church as to how our Third Article of Faith must be worded in Danish, so that we thereby express neither more nor less than our faith in the Holy Spirit in every part of the Holy Church or the Holy Universal congregation of people, the Community of Saints, with the forgiveness of sins, the resurrection of the body and life everlasting.

Once the Church knows this, then it hardly needs enlightenment from us to see that the word 'Church' and every other obscure word that has been substituted for 'congregation' or 'assembly' has done very great damage, both by obscuring the relationship between the Church and the Spirit, and as a loophole for the Pope and all those who, like the masters of the faith, wish to replace the Holy Spirit with themselves, or at least be considered the only ones to possess the Holy Spirit and thus be intermediaries between the Spirit and the Church.

Likewise the Church will then be ready for the further enlightenment which, according to the other words of institution both at baptism and Holy Communion and according to the Apostles' writings, we can and must give on the working of the Holy Spirit. As Luther has already noted in his interpretation of our Third Article of Faith, this begins with the preaching of the Gospel and does not end until the whole Church, also bodily, is glorified in everlasting life.

At this point we must first note that the Holy Spirit, which accomplishes the Divine purpose in the Church and in whose name we are baptized just as much as in 'the name of the Father and of the Son', must not be assumed to be merely a power or some sort of angel. Rather it is what has been called a divine person, that is: the power of the Most High, which is conscious of itself and which dispenses to each as It will, that is: in a divine way It is independent and free.

Now what is true of all spirits, even of the spiritual larva, which is the soul in us, namely that they are invisible and can only reveal themselves in the invisible word through the power they invest in it and the effect they thereby produce amongst any spiritually receptive group, large or small, this is now also true of the spirit of the Lord and His Church, the Holy Spirit, which proceeds from the Father. So, learning to distinguish the Holy Spirit and Its purpose from all erring and inferior spirits is a question of knowing a Word through which It works, thereby revealing Its spiritual power, just as each one of us reveals his spiritual power or his spiritual impotence in his words, and just as every nation's spirit reveals its power in its mother tongue. And this is the dynamic Word of the Holy Spirit in which It reveals Itself and through which It accomplishes Its whole divine purpose amongst us. This is Christ's gospel or His good tidings as it is powerfully expressed in the Word from Our Lord Jesus Christ's own mouth at His divine institutions – Holy Baptism, Holy Communion and first and foremost in the Word of Faith which everybody has to confess at baptism and must believe in order to be taken into His Church by Our Lord through baptism.

So only where this Word of Faith, baptism and communion is heard undistorted in its rightful place and in its rightful context, only there can we find the Spirit of Our Lord Jesus Christ, only amongst those who in their heart of hearts believe this Word, only amongst them does He accomplish His purpose; and only those preachers of the gospel in whose sermons the Word of the Lord Himself is the soul, only they are moved by the Spirit of the Lord, only they are His instruments for rightful service in the Church of the Lord.

That this Spirit of Our Lord Jesus Christ which does not speak Its own words but only what It hears, and which makes the Word of the Lord a divine witness for us by turning it to spirit and life for us; that this is what we call with the Word of the Lord at Baptism the Holy Spirit, the spirit of holiness or of purity of heart and truth – can never be accepted by a world that does not believe in Our Lord Jesus Christ. And it is no use quarrelling with the world about this, since it can only be proved in the course of time among and for the believers by the effect of the Spirit on their hearts. So that what the Spirit of Our Lord Jesus Christ can prove, has proved and every day does prove to the world is only that It is a Spirit above all spirits. The Spirit of the Lord proved this clearly through Its first revelation at Pentecost when It endowed the Apostles with the ability to explain Christ's gospel with vigour and power to all nations in their own tongue. But the Spirit of Our Lord has further proved this in the course of time, and proves it every day far more profoundly by taking possession of every nation's tongue wherever the true gospel of Christ through baptism and Holy Communion according to the Lord's own institution is preached and is heard, so that His instruments can then speak with far more vigour and power about Jesus Christ and all that is His than the instruments of the national spirit have been able to speak about the nation itself and about its heroes and demigods and its particular faith, hope and charity. However, this divine continuation and verification of the Whitsun miracle with the burning tongues is still hidden from the majority of Christians because their natural way of thinking has been contaminated by the spiritual death of the world, since it is selv-evident that when one has no feeling for the spirit of one's own nation and tongue as the vital spark in the language and thoughts of invisible things within us and above us, that is, divine and human things, then no parallel can be drawn between this spirit and the Spirit of Our Lord Jesus Christ and His Church. Nor therefore is it as yet much use writing for the Church about what it means to be gathered up and born of the Spirit of the Lord through faith and baptism into a new Israel, into a spiritual nation of God, as exalted above all the nations of the world as the Lord is exalted above all lords and His Spirit above all spirits. Nor is it much use writing about the community of Saints fostered by the Spirit of the

Lord through the Lord's Prayer and at the Lord's table, which also surpasses the warmest fellowship between earthly parents and children, brothers and sisters, friends and husbands and wives to the same degree as the love of God and Our Lord Jesus Christ surpasses all our natural human love. For in order to appreciate this we must first come to know the natural spirit of our nation and our natural love in their best guises, where the flesh admittedly plays the greater part but where nevertheless there can and must be so much spirituality and warmth of feeling that we derive from it a living yardstick that can and must teach us to appreciate the incomparable power and love to be found in the Spirit of God's people and in the heart of the Christian brotherhood.

There may well be better ways of writing about the gifts of the Holy Spirit in Our Lord Jesus Christ's name to the whole Church and its fellowship, since each of us who feels he is a sinner also feels that he is in great need of forgiveness, and learns that it cannot be found anywhere except within the Church of Our Lord Jesus Christ; and each of us who feels his mortality has also learnt something of the bitterness of death, and knows that no herb grows against this except within God's Paradise and that there is no comfort except in the hope of eternal life both for the soul and for the body. But as long as we have no living feeling of our admission to the people of God and of our incorporation into the Community of Saints, then we cannot have an adequate conviction of the forgiveness of sins, the resurrection of the body and an everlasting life given by the Holy Spirit. For It is not sent to any individual but to the whole Church, and does not grant forgiveness of sins and eternal life to any of us individually but only to each and every one of us in the Church which It gathers and in the fellowship It creates.

On the other hand, we can and must impress upon the believers, by word of mouth and in writing, that a major obstacle to the awareness of their Church and their feeling of a warm fellowship can only be swept aside by the Creed, Baptism and Holy Communion according to the Lord's institution becoming, secularly and socially speaking, a completely free matter; so that far from wanting to lure or threaten anyone into a confession of their faith, to rebirth in the Lord's Baptism and fellowship at the Lord's Table, the believing Christian must on the contrary warn everyone and implore them under no circumstances to lie to God by confessing a faith they do not have, or by deriding the Lord's means to salvation, as they do when without believing in the Father, Son and Holy Spirit they allow themselves to be baptized in the name of the Trinity and without the desire of faith for the warm fellowship with Our Lord Jesus Christ and all His friends they unworthily eat His body and drink His blood. Only then can it be brought to light again that the Lord has bought those who believe and are baptized as His own chosen people, and that at His table He teaches all his friends to love one another as He loves His.

It is therefore very sad that amongst us there are still many believers who are frightened of freedom and thus refuse the Lord's Spirit which calls us all in freedom and can never be revealed except in freedom, since all spiritual bondage of necessity obscures and hides Its work. For when one hears millions confessing the word of faith and being baptized and fed with the words of grace and eternal life without its effect being seen on them, but rather that their enslavement to sin and death, as miserable as it is ungodly, is quite unmistakable, then it becomes impossible to place any faith in this word, containing the Spirit of God and to preserve one's faith, unless one opens one's eyes to the reprehensible mockery which is perpetrated in the name of the Creed and with the sacraments, when it is attempted in this manner to force God's gifts on to someone or sneak them into him – gifts that are only handed out by His free mercy and can only become theirs if they receive them from the hand of the Lord with free faith and gratitude.

In fact, not until we fervently regret instead of defending the mess that secular Christianity and Church discipline have created, can we in the midst of the confusion begin to catch a glimpse of God's path on earth and His course to salvation for all people; so that in all of those, be they few or many, who truly say 'yes' to the Baptismal Covenant and seek a rebirth in baptism, in them all He begins His good work through the forgiveness of sins, without which no rebirth to eternal life is possible, for the wages of sin is death. But rebirth follows of necessity from the forgiveness of sins, for when Our Lord forgives us all our sins, then He shows us His mercy, just as a father can show mercy to his reprobate but penitent children, and God's mercy must be the source of eternal life, as it is written: the Wages of sin is death but God's gift of grace is eternal life through Our Lord Jesus Christ. However, since it is just as much in the name of Our Lord Jesus Christ as for His sake and through the Word of His mouth alone that we can have forgiveness of sins, the resurrection of the flesh and eternal life, so it is not until at the Table of Our Lord, through the words of His mouth that give us a share in His, for us, sacrificed body and His blood shed for us for the forgiveness of sins, that the Spirit of the Lord in our loving fellowship (koinonia in Greek and communio in Latin) with the Lord and one another allows us to feel the blessed certainty that all our sins were obliterated when the writing that condemned us was nailed, together with Our Lord Jesus Christ, to His cross, and that in His love we have passed from death into life; so that the death of the body, even if we have to suffer it, will not harm us but be triumphantly defeated by our resurrection in 'flesh and bone' in the name of our crucified Lord, who rose thus from the grave for our sake.

Not until we thus link our faith and our creed to baptism and Holy Communion as the Lord's means of grace to the great work of redemption and salvation, will we feel that the Spirit of the Lord, the eternal life-force, is becoming active in us, so that we can grow in the grace and knowledge of Our Lord Jesus Christ.

For just as the good tidings that out of His great love God has sacrificed His only begotten Son, that whosoever believeth in Him should not perish but have everlastig life, do not enlighten us until we learn through the Word of Faith at baptism both what sort of God it is that loves us so much and who His only begotten Son sacrificed for us really is, and what it means to believe in Him, and how we are then saved from perdition, and how we thus gain eternal life; so the good tidings do not become spirit and life for us until they come living and warm to us from Our Lord's own mouth, something which the written word neither is nor ever can be, but only derives from and points to; and now it is clearly our Third Article of Faith again, or our Creed's confession of the Holy Spirit and Its work, through which life has come to us. For only in the Spirit is God with us, and only through the Spirit does God work among us, from Ascension Day to Judgement Day; so that however firmly we believe in the Father and the Son, as the Creed goes, it is of necessity a dead faith if we do not believe in the Holy Spirit. For it is the Spirit alone which quickens and accomplishes everything the Father has promised us, and what the only begotten Son has earned and bought for us. Therefore, just as the new life in Christ Jesus has always become weaker and darker to the extent that belief in the Holy Spirit faltered and the Third Article of Faith was obscured, so the future will also prove that the new life in Christ grows stronger and brighter to the extent that belief in the Holy Spirit is strengthened and our Third Article of Faith is illuminated in us.

To all those who follow this rule, as the servant of the Lord I say with the Apostle: Peace and Mercy are upon them!

Notes

This essay is chapter III of Elementary Christian Teachings and was first published in 1855.

1. See introduction to Elementary Christian Teachings.
2. Grundtvig refers to Martin Luther's Shorter Catechism (1529).

The Christian Signs of Life

For as long as Christianity has existed in the world every serious-minded person who has felt attracted to it as being the divine truth has also felt that the question of salvation cannot possibly be an integral part of eternal life without having an appreciable influence on the temporal life of man. Thus, whoever actually denies this and expects from Christianity only a 'blessed death', thereby both reveals his spiritual death and exposes Christianity to the bitter and obviously well-deserved scorn of the unbelieving world. For if Christ's gospel was no more than a so-called 'word of eternal life' that made the temporal human life even deader than it was before, then no truth-loving person either could or need believe in such a gospel. For whatever is without spirit or spiritually dead and powerless in time cannot possibly be full of spirit or spiritually all-powerful in eternity. To this end Our Lord Jesus Christ Himself has borne witness that we must be spiritually reborn in the course of our temporal life in order to have a share in the eternal life, and that this is a truth about life on earth that must be believed before one can believe the truth about the life in heaven.

Therefore, although the papists' concept of Christianity was as spiritually dead and powerless as could be without being clearly self-contradictory, yet even the papists themselves sternly insisted on a so-called Christian way of life, that is the monastic life, which was to be regarded as the property of the whole Church, in which every member could have a share by believing it and by contributing, each according to his ability, to the maintenance, welfare and glorification of this so-called godly and Christian monastic life. However, the fact that this monastic life, even with the halo of a saintly life around it, was from a spiritual and Christian point of view only a shadowy life that revealed the very spiritual death that it sought to hide, has been so clearly exposed that it requires no further evidence, at least not amongst Martin Luther's disciples.

Now as regards these disciples of Martin Luther, or the Lutherans, so called, there is no denying that they erred badly in what they said and wrote when they maintained, as if they meant it, that the temporal life of man, as in fact ungodly and irredeemable, must be cancelled out in the name of salvation, and that we must think only about a 'blessed death'; for as the Ecclesiast says, 'The day of death is better than the day of one's birth'.[1] Now since, like their Calvinist counterparts the Lutheran doctrinal systems were based on the dead letter and on the concept of scripture, and since the academic life of our scribes was obviously even less godly than that of the monks, the papists could with some show of justification accuse us of having an even deader concept of Christianity than they had themselves. But even so, the Lutherans had still made the better choice and had lined up on the side of life, for they left the spiritually dead shadowy life to the papists and took comfort in the spirit which, despite their life of apparent death, could and would make them alive with Christ.

In the midst of their unjustifiable condemnation of the entire natural life of man and their eulogies over the 'blessed death' and the 'blessed corpses', the Lutherans nevertheless demanded in earnest a living faith for true Christianity, a faith that should demonstrate its spiritual power and its reality in a spoken confession of faith, preaching of the gospel and song of praise in the mother tongue. And we make bold to declare that with these words we have named the proper Christian signs of life, which must never be entirely absent wherever there is true Christianity, nor can ever be found together except where the quickening Spirit of the Lord is the congregation's divine advocate, its comforter and companion guide to all truth.

What nevertheless made ever the sincere Lutherans' apparently dead in their daily life and stunted the growth of their Christian life was their confused and self-contradictory way of thinking about evangelical freedom together with enslavement under a State church, rebirth in baptism together with faith and life according to scripture, and finally the Christian renewal of human life without a previous human life to be renewed. So that when we now with God's help see light in the light of the Lord, then the confession of faith will be much firmer and fuller, the preaching of the gospel simpler and more powerful, and the song of praise much clearer and more beautiful, and the whole of our temporal human life will thereby be given a revitalized form in heart and spirit. The

Christian quality of this form though it cannot be strictly proved is certain enough, for this noble, heartfelt form of life will only be found where the Christian confession of faith, preaching of the gospel and hymn of praise flourish. Admittedly we have recently seen that this enlightenment is still a rarity among us, for when Søren Kierkegaard a moment[2] ago tried to frighten the life out of us with his charcoal drawing of the 'Begging Monk" as the only true disciple of Christ, who literally carried his cross on his back and followed him, then he was met as usual with crass ignorance about the Christian life. Yet, fortunately he found in the corners the morning light, which will lend glory to life, and which was urged on by the black rain-cloud to vigorous strides forward on its heroic path.[3]

On this particular occasion it became quite clear that all disputes and discussions about the Christian life are just so much talk if we do not presuppose and maintain that the Christian congregation, created by baptism according to the Lord's own institution, has its own peculiar life-spring in this alone, and that the congregation's confession of faith at baptism is therefore the only Christian confession and, as the living expression of the Christian faith, is both the first and the last sign of Christian life. On the other hand, given this fundamental knowledge about Christian life as a life of faith and about the confession of faith in the congregation as the essential true sign of life, we can clearly see that it is only in a living preaching of the gospel and song of praise that accords with the confession of faith that the Christian life can and must continually show itself more powerfully and more openly, whilst the whole course of the Christian Church must demonstrate whether the new Christian life is more or less human than the old one, either as it was led before Christ came or as it is lived without the baptismal faith in Christ or the rebirth to His own human life in baptism according to His own institution.

One might now make bold to assert that our elementary Christian teachings conflict with scripture because the debate about the true meaning of the words of men now dead is an endless one and also because book-knowledge and scripture-knowledge are and must be so vastly different from one another that even if all Christians were clever readers only very few of them would have a solidly based conviction either about the biblical character of Christianity or about the Christian character of the Bible. We Christian scribes however will triumphantly defend the claim that our Holy Scripture, far from denying our elementary Christian Teachings about 'faith and baptism', is in fact in total agreement with them, and offers in particular the creed as the primary Christian sign of life, a glorious witness, in the words of the Lord, 'Whosoever shall confess me before men, him shall the son of man also confess before the angels of God".[4]

Now, just as of necessity we must first and last give the same weight to the creed outwardly as we give to faith inwardly, since the confession of faith in the new life corresponds to breathing in the old, yet it is far from our purpose thereby to exclude either the preaching of the gospel or the song of praise, which are also signs of life that can as little be excluded where the Christian life is to grow and prosper as the life that is born of faith can thrive and mature without the corresponding hope and love. This hope and this love have the same relationship to the living preaching of the gospel as faith has to the living confession of faith. So that where the creed is the only sign of life, there the life of faith will always be found, weak and sickly and in every trial fighting for life. This is further explained by the fact that not only did the Christian faith first enter this world through the preaching of Him who came from above and in truth spoke the 'Word of God' but also the faith is transmitted, according to the Apostle's express testimony, only through the living profession of the Word of Faith; so he asks not only 'How then shall they call on him in whom they have not believed?' but also, and equally importantly, 'How shall they hear without a preacher?'.[5]

So despite the fact that the Christian confession of faith can be found alive and still is alive, wherever in general the preaching of the gospel amongst the congregation may be said to be extinct, there the confession will either soon die out and take faith to the grave with it, or it will gain in power so as to bear again the living preaching of the gospel, as it undoubtedly did in and through Martin Luther.

For what actually was the case with us at the beginning of the nineteenth century was apparently the case throughout most of the Christian world at the beginning of the sixteenth century, so that the living preaching of the Word of Faith was to human eyes either totally extinct, or was so obviously moribund that in order for it to continue to transmit the faith from generation to generation it had to be miraculously reborn. And clearly reborn it was, in and through Martin Luther, who again with spirit and life preached the ancient Word of Faith in the mother tongue of his people, and thus revived the preaching of the gospel not only amongst the kindred tribes in England and the three Nordic kingdoms but even to a certain degree amongst the Latin nations, as can be seen everywhere, but most obviously with the Calvinists.

What was proved by this miraculous event was not so much 'the universal priesthood' – as the Calvinists thought, since Martin Luther was himself ordained, but rather the rebirth of the preaching of the gospel in him proved that the Christian priesthood has just as little an exclusive authority or sole right to the preaching of the Gospel as it has any spiritual control over the Lord's institutions.

For when Martin Luther, far from attributing the slightest part of his calling to his ordination or his ability to preach the Gospel but on the contrary rejecting any claim that the ordination be regarded as a sacrament to believers, it obviously could not be an inherent part of his ordination that the living preaching of the Gospel should be reborn through him, whilst this rebirth of the preaching of the gospel is indeed a far greater and recognisable miracle of God than the regular continuation of the preaching of the gospel can ever be.

Although ordination may therefore be what I truly believe it to be in spite of Luther's denial – namely the Spirit's sacrament for the Christian scribes who believe in it, ordination cannot possibly, in spite of the Lutheran evidence, give the slightest lustre to any popery or hierarchy of priests. Here it is a question of understanding the Apostle correctly when, speaking of the preaching of the Word, he asks: 'How shall they preach except they be sent?'[6] On the one hand we are led by this almost to think of an outward, visible commission, like ordination with its laying-on of hands, but on the other hand the Apostle Paul cannot have been thinking exclusively of this since he himself was an exception and often asserts his exceptional position in being sent out in a manner known only to himself by the ascended Lord Himself to preach the Gospel with His Spirit. Now, since Martin Luther, as we know, generally had a very Pauline idea of the Christian life, it is understandable enough that in front of the Pope and his miscreant priests he supported with a certain one-sidedness the Pauline commissioning. Of course we cannot condone this indefensible one-sidedness by which an exception is made into a rule, and in fact on behalf of the Apostle Paul we must make the objection against Martin Luther that not

154

only did the Apostle allow himself to be ordained as a missionary with the laying-on of hands, but he also expressly attributes a priestly gift of the Spirit to the laying-on of hands by the Elders; and finally he admits there is a special commissioning to baptize which he did not have. But even with all this the fact still remains that the ascended Lord has reserved the right, without any human mediation, to commission preachers with the Spirit. When they themselves have been baptized they have the right to baptize whoever they will, so that no priesthood, however genuinely apostolic it may be, can have a Christian basis for claiming a monopoly either to preach the Gospel or to baptize; that is to say, they cannot demand a Christian right to spiritual control either over the Christian light or the Christian life. An awareness of this may, indeed must, under certain circumstances produce what is known amongst us as 'revivals' and 'godly assemblies', the quality of whose Christianity must therefore in no way be denied on behalf of the priesthood as being an unacceptable lay activity, but must be judged, just like the priest's office, by the relationship to the Christian confession of faith and song of praise in an indissoluble union with Holy Baptism, which through rebirth opens up the Christian life-springs – and with Holy Communion, which in community with the word itself creates and sustains the Christian stream of life.

For just as the congregation's confession of faith at baptism is the undeviating rule for all Christian confession and must be the core of all Christian preaching of the Gospel, so must all Christian life be derived exclusively from the Lord's own deeds with the words of His mouth at the Holy Communion and at baptism. And only by elevating the Christian life in connection with this does the congregation's song of praise become Christian. Therefore, just as it is a sure sign of spiritual death amongst the Papists that the song of praise in the mother-tongue has been dropped, so is the Lutheran song of praise in the mother tongue a clear sign of life and a valid witness to the Christian character of the Lutheran preaching, since the song of praise will always correspond to the preaching because it is with the hymn of praise that the congregation respond on the address. That is way the Calvinist preaching in the mother-tongue also gave birth to a corresponding song of praise, but only in a Jewish, not in a Christian form, thereby denying the Christian life to the Calvinist teaching, nor, on account of its superior attitude to the life-spring in baptism and the life-stream in Communion, did it have the best claim to that life. For so long as baptism and communion are regarded only as shadowy images either of circumcision and the paschal lamb or of the spiritual rebirth and the staff of life, then they stop themselves from crossing the Red Sea dryshod, and going straight into the Promised Land!

Admittedly the Lutheran preaching and song of praise had their flaws and their deficiencies, as they did not relate 'faith' to the Word of Faith clearly or vividly enough and would not therefore clearly and vividly enough help the Christian life in its spring and outflow of the Lord's own words and actions at baptism and communion. But because the Lutheran preaching and song of praise, however dimly, presupposed and actively asserted the real presence and life-giving power of God's Word through the Lord's own institutions, the Christian life still revealed itself more powerfully and more clearly through them than had been the case for many centuries. Since the faults in the Lutheran preaching of the gospel and song of praise have now corrected themselves, so to speak, or rather have allowed themselves to be corrected by the spirit in the congregation's confession of faith and the life within the Lord's words of institution, we have the right to claim that the faults had their root in the lack of light and power that the infant is not accountable for; since it goes without saying that the new-born Christian preaching and the congregation's song of praise in the days of Martin Luther and on his lips were only in their infancy.

This perhaps illustrates best how obstructive and inappropriate any doctrinal ordinances but Holy Writ, be they orthodox altar books or hymnaries, have been and must be for the living development of Lutheran preaching and song of praise in a Christian direction, because even in its most tolerable forms all that can only be compared to a meagrely apportioned and monotonous fare. This may be considered necessary in old age, it may prevent feverish illnesses and may even delay death for a while; but in childhood it will be far more likely to weaken vitality , prevent physical development and stunt the growth of the child. If, therefore, those two wonderful children of Luther, the reborn Christian preaching and song of praise in each nation's own mother tongue, are to grow to maturity in the power of the Spirit and to their glory become immortal on earth, as we hope and pray they will, then we must disregard all the sulks and frowns of the dullards and give a free rein to the preaching of the gospel and the song of praise in accord with the Spirit's impulse within in the boundaries of the creed. For this is the true 'evangelical freedom', the freedom in Paradise to eat from all of the trees in the garden except the Tree of Death, which is the sort of scribe-knowledge and theology that puts itself in Our Lord's place in order to judge His words and deeds: His Word to us and what He works within us. For as soon as we give up building on and resting in the witness of the Spirit and the Church to the Christian faith and creed and to the Lord's institutions as his own deeds together with the Word of God which He Himself actually is and which He alone has within His power, and instead call into question this foundation of the faith and the very source of the Church's life (the rock with its spring), and make proud under whatever name we choose in the seat of judgement, to decide for ourselves whether we really do have a living Word of God amongst us, whether that Word of God is true and good in every way, and whether it really can accomplish great things such as purifying the soul and making life out of death, then we are standing like Eve beside the forbidden tree, holding court with the serpent on which fruits are pleasant and good to acquire knowledge of good and evil: just as the Scripture says, 'But I fear, lest by any means, as the serpent beguiled Eve through his subtlety, so your minds should be corrupted from the simplicity that is in Christ.'[7]

If from this angle and on this path we now approach the question of the individual's Christian certainty of his salvation, which has recently been dragged into the quarrel on the Christian validity of baptism administered according to the ritual of the altar-book,[8] then the same thing happens as with all questions of Christian enlightenment; namely, that although we do not find it adequately answered in any doctrinal system, we nevertheless do find here the great Lutheran principle for Christian enlightenment (these principles of the Word and the faith) as fruitful as it is unshakable. Admittedly the papists are right to claim that the individual must build his guarantee of salvation on his participation in the faith, hope and charity of the whole Christian Church, so that it was Martin Luther's great venture to direct every soul in particular to the inner witness of the Holy Spirit as the only token of God's grace and everlasting life; yet, on the other hand, this venture had been made necessary by the deadness with which the priestly hierarchy and compulsory baptism had smitten the very concept of 'the Church'. For just as God is not the God of the dead but the

God of the living, so is the Holy Spirit not the spirit of the dead Church, but the spirit of the living Church alone. Thus it is a totally false and pernicious conviction of salvation that people draw from their certainty of having membership of a spiritually dead Church, in which the Christian means to salvation and the Christian necessities of life (baptism and communion) are either corrupted or are at any rate not alive and working. For a dead Church such as this is only a self-made "spiritual fire insurance society" which, in return for a formal payment and an annual subscription undertakes to guarantee its members against all spiritual fire damage both in purgatory and in hell-fire. Martin Luther was right when he said that all those guarantees that such a spiritual fire office could give either to avoid hell or to enter into heaven are nothing but fraud and murder of the spirit. And when Luther constantly referred to that external and clear Word of God through which we can and must get to know and understand the Holy Spirit, then his mistake lay, as it did throughout his evangelical work, only in the fact that he confused all his biblical preaching with the confession of faith and the Words of Institution, at if all of it was an altogether clear Word of God which enabled us to get to know and understand the Holy Spirit. Therefore, as soon as we learn to separate what only we and not Our Lord has joined together, so that the congregation's confession of faith at baptism according to the Lord's institution becomes the clear hallmark both of the Church and its Spirit. then it will become obvious that we, as members of this Church, as the Christian and spiritual people of God, can get the same certainty on the question of our salvation as the Church has through its awareness of the Christian signs of life in the confession of faith, the preaching of the gospel and the song of praise. It is equally obvious that these signs of life will grow stronger and stronger, both in general and in detail, the freer the confession of faith, the preaching of gospel, and the song of praise are, whilst every external constraint against the Spirit's preserves of necessity both weakens the manifestations of life and conceals the signs of life. For just as no one can be completely sure of the sincerity and stability of their Christian confession of faith when this confession is a civic injunction and its opposite a civic offence, so the Christian preaching of the gospel and the congregation's song of praise can never become the strong and clear manifestations and signs of life that give a spiritual guarantee of life strength and growth unless they are completely free from external constraint. So that whoever sets himself against the freedom of the clergy and the freedom of the hymn book sets himself, wittingly or unwittingly, just as much against every sure certainty of salvation as against that spirit which only works with freedom in freedom and for the glorious freedom in every way of God's children. On the other hand wherever all things spiritual are free, there we can boldly say to every believer who questions us about the validity of his baptism: 'Why ask me? Ask the Holy Spirit'. He who is the spirit of both faith and baptism will at once tell you if you were born of water and spirit to enter into the Kingdom of Heaven, and if you are not, he will both urge you and show you the way to be so.

Notes

This essay is chapter nine of "Elementary Christian teachings" and was first published in 1857.
1. Ecclesiastes 4.2. Grundtvig does not give the exact wording of the Bible.
2. Grundtvig refers to Søren Kierkegaard's attack on Christianity in "Training in Christianity" (1850) and in "The Instant" (1855).
3. Grundtvig refers to his feeling that his view of Christianity was beginning to find acceptance in the Church, which Kierkegaard certainly did not approve of.
4. Luke 12.18.
5. Rom. 10.14.
6. II Cor. 11.39.
7. Grundtvig refers to his own polemic with Jakob Peter Mynster (1775-1854) whose proposal for a new altarbook including a revision of the wording of the ritual at baptism Grundtvig strongly opposed.

VII

Sermons

Except for short intervals N. F. S. Grundtvig was active as a preacher in the Danish Church from 1811 to the day before his death in 1872. The body of some 3000 sermons is consequently the biggest province of his literary legacy. Here it is possible, Sunday by Sunday, to follow the development of his thinking in almost every field. Naturally the sermons are particularly important for an appreciation of the development of his theology. A remarkable feature of his preaching is that some sermons may be described as prose poems and phrased accordingly, that is, they represent an intermediary stage between prose proper and poetry in regular metre. Finally it is typical of Grundtvig that many of his theological insights or "discoveries" will turn up in poetic contexts before they appear in his conscious theological reasoning.

An example of his prose poetry is the sermon for the sixteenth Sunday after Trinity 1823. The formal text for the sermon is Eph. 3, 13-21, but, in fact, it is rather Ps. 27 (as is clear from the preamble) and the Gospel for the day: the reviving of the widow's son at Nain (Luke 7, 11-17), as well as the story of Dives and Lazarus (Luke, 16-31). The theme is the human condition; man has an innate longing for eternity, that is, for God. It is depicted in dark colours with an awareness of the reality of death, which man will not face. But as the sermon progresses, the longing for eternity becomes a hallmark of man's nobility: man is not simply a flower but a "wonderful flower" as he reaches out for God, for it is this longing and this hope that are raised from the dead at the behest of the Gospel corresponding to Christ's word to the mourning widow.

Grundtvig's development over the years, following after, may be learned from the second example, the sermon for the same Sunday in 1836 over the same text (Luke 7, 11-17). The sermon has the telling heading and theme: Weep not! It is an empty word when spoken by man, but the very meaning and essence of the Gospel when spoken by Almighty God. Weep not! was, to be true, spoken by Christ to his disciples at the time; when it is heard now, it is a witness to his living presence in the Church. The "Weep not", now heard in the Church, is Christ's personal address in the service – at baptism when the Lord himself asks, "Do you believe?" and draws the child into His Kingdom, and in communion when it is spoken as a command, "Take, eat ... Drink ye all of it." The baptism and communion now taking place, is an essence of the "Weep not" which was spoken by Christ. The sermon is a simple statement of what has been called Grundtvig's ecclesiastical view, that God is above all present in the sacraments during worship.

During his lifetime Grundtvig published "Biblical Sermons" in 1816 and "The Sunday Book", containing three volumes of sermons, which appeared 1827-1831. Apart from books of selections made after his death from time to time, the bulk of the sermons have remained unpublished. They are now appearing in a critical edition, which will run to twelve volumes.

Chr. Thodberg

Sermon for Evensong on 16th Sunday in Trinity 1823:
Luke 7:11-17

One thing have I desired of the Lord,
that will I seek after;
that I may dwell in the house of the Lord
all the days of my life,
to behold the beauty of the Lord
and to enquire in his temple.[1]
Thus sings David,
the man with the sweet psalm-tongue in Israel,
and the song of the sons of Korah answers loud and clear:
My soul longeth, yea, even fainteth for the courts of the Lord:[2]
For a day in thy courts is better than a thousand
I had rather be a doorkeeper in the house of my God
than to dwell in the tents of wickedness.[3]

When we listen reverently to such tones
the heart cannot help but ask
what sort of house is this,
where is it to be found,
cannot the gate to these courts,
cannot the door to these rooms
be opened for me too,
so that I may learn to feel
the blessed joy the psalms breathe.
So the heart sighs
and beseeches with the psalmist:
O God, send out thy light and thy truth:
that they may lead me,
let them bring me
unto thy holy hill, and to thy tabernacles.
Then will I go in unto God,
my exceeding joy:
yea, upon the harp will I praise thee,
O God, my God![4]

Truly, my friends!
Once the heart has learnt
to ask and then to sigh
in the deep awareness
that in none of the dwelling-places
that men build
is there constancy,
is there peace and happiness
without fear and without loss;
and that in all of them, even the brightest,
there are gloomy corners
where the night-owl lives
and spreads the terror of the night;
and that all are of the dust,
and all turn to dust again,[5]
as the best of all visible dwelling-places,
the earthly work for the Eternal,
the works of His hands in the dust,
this wonderful human body
in His image
in which the living invisible lives
which we call ourselves,
which finds expression in the word
that passes across our lips,
and treads its invisible, wonderful path,
flying as a thought-bird
from spirit to spirit,
from heart to heart.

Truly, once the heart has become
acquainted with its longings,
its deep longing for a quiet habitation,[6]
that shall not be taken down,
whose stakes shall never be removed,
and whose cords shall never be broken,
once the heart has become
acquainted with these longings,
which may for a time be strange to us,
but which slumber in the chamber of every heart,
and will awake one day, if not before

then on the day this habitation is broken down by death,
and each of us is alone with himself
with the invisible
that seeks and sorrows and sighs,
that is afflicted in its tabernacle[7]
and will awake, if not before
then one day — like the rich man in the gospel
when in pain he lifted up his eyes,
and saw the yawning gulf between himself
and the house of rest in Abraham's bosom —[8]
Once the heart has become acquainted with these longings,
then the sigh,
as deep as desire,
mounts up to Him
who dwells in the hidden light
in the glory from which all dust is barred,
whose rays we behold everywhere,
wherever the eye turns,
whose warmth we feel in our innermost being,
whose flame lights up our breast
and lifts up our eyes to heaven
leads us in every thought, to the Eternal
in every longing and in every sigh.

Oh Man, do you know what this means?
Has your ear understood it
and have you heard its echo in your heart?
Do you know the house
that is sung about in Israel
whose praises are so loudly extolled in Zion's hymn of praise?
Do you know the House of the Lord
that hovered before David's eyes,
that aroused in his soul those deep longings,
and whose beauty he cannot praise enough,
wishing for an eternity
to gaze upon and see beyond it,
whose loveliness flowed through his heart
and poured out of his lips
in the sweet and blissful tones.

Yes or no –
how shall I answer for you, my friends!
Yes or no –
your lives will answer for you
though your lips be still,
and, consider this, they will tell the truth
though your tongue lie
and your heart deceive itself,
they will tell the truth
and He who sees in secret
He shall hear it and He shall judge –
If your eyes are nailed to this earth
by worldly pleasures,
if it is here you seek your heaven for your rest
your peace, your joy,
if with your spirit and your hand
you pile dust upon dust
to build yourself a house that can glitter and sparkle
houses that can stand,
houses that can hold and increase your happiness
if that is your endeavour
and greatest pleasure
then you do not know the desire
that tuned David's harp
nor the house,
up to whose balcony its notes soar.

But, O Man!
If you know nothing of this
what do you know at all?
What else do you know
apart from what is today
and perishes tomorrow?
What do you know
of all that you saw
of all that hovered before you
within and without?
What do you know other than the outer garment,
the ephemeral, passing form?
What is your life's achievement,

what is your day's work,
what have you wrought and thought?
What is it but childishness
ridiculous beyond belief
when it is taken seriously,
when the prime of life
when the course of all your days is taken up with it?
What do you build on
except a house of cards
which the breath of Time overturns in the next moment?
What are you fighting against
except your own shadow,
which you deceive yourself into thinking you have beaten
as it passes behind you,
whence comes your joy
but from the shining bubbles that burst in the air
before you can even fix your eyes upon them?
What is your whole life
but smoke, a vapour, that vanisheth away?[9]
What are you, with your greatest gifts
in your finest splendour
with your health and strength
with honour and power
with riches and wisdom
with all this what are you
but a flower,
a strange flower,
planted by an unseen hand on this earth
only to disappear in a little while
and to confirm by your fall
that dust is man's kinsman?
What is your pleasure and your pain,
your rest and your unrest,
your joy and your sorrow,
when all that you build upon must fall,
when all that you love must die,
when all that you think is vanity,
when the finest house you know
is the wonderful but frail tabernacle
in which you found yourself,
in which you dwell and move,

in which you think and speak,
you, the invisible, the intangible
living human soul?
What are you then
if this body,
this tabernacle,
is the highest, the best, the loveliest
the sweetest house you know?
What are you
when it is destroyed,
and you know that it must be destroyed,
perhaps today, perhaps tomorrow,
and even in the longest life
still one of the days that soon can be numbered,
in one of the years that children name
as they sit on your lap and count to a hundred?
You know that of that building
There shall not be left here one stone upon another,
one bone with another,
that shall not be thrown down.[10]
These limbs shall have no joints left
But shall be parted, dissolved and crumbled to dust.

And what then,
you may protest,
What then?
Believing that this building,
this my body's tabernacle,[11]
the loveliest, the happiest house I know
probably also is the most glorious,
the loveliest house to be found —
or rather, which I can find.
What use is it that I delude myself
that there is a better house, a loftier
brighter, more permanent house, an everlasting house,
and tortured myself desiring it?
And even destroyed the grain of joy
that came my way
embittering the very span of days
allotted to me.

170

Fools, lying fools!
What are you trying to say?
Why must you lie against the truth?
For you know very well,
you must know,
that the desire for the house
that is eternal and has an everlasting loveliness,
the desire for a quiet tabernacle
that shall not be taken down,
whose stakes shall never be removed,
and whose cords shall never be broken,[12]
you know very well
that this desire dwells in your breast
even when it makes no sound;
you know very well
where it lies sleeping in the gloomy chamber of the heart,
and every time you quite rightly rejoiced over life
and found a dwelling-place where you wanted to build,
then you yourself awakened it with your wish
that this building might never be destroyed,
that this happiness might last for ever;
you awakened it and could not do otherwise,
even though you learnt each time
that you thereby called forth more torment for yourself
called forth the worm that smote your gourd[13]
and bit the flower of your happiness
so that it withered and died.

Therefore never speak of avoiding these longings,
the deep longings for the house,
built without hands,
built on the eternal heights,
secure against flood and storm,
and which possesses an everlasting loveliness!
Never speak of it!
Never deny that you know them
nor deny that they torment you
embittering your days and destroying your happiness
for as long as you fail to find the abode of your desires
the permanent tabernacle,

and see the door ajar,
see it open for you too.
Never deny it!
For God knows you are lying,
and all of us
who have learnt from your word
that in this house of flesh and bone that we behold
there lives an invisible one, as it lives in us,
a living soul that is created like ours
and in whom our Word finds an echo.
Never deny it,
O Man, whoever you may be!
And if you would take the only useful advice,
then do not hate this longing
for the everlasting, for the eternal,
however much it torments you;
learn rather to love it and believe
that what is the highest and deepest in you
can only be the best.
Open your eyes
and see what is so crystal clear –
that this longing that tormented you
which you hated, fought against and could never conquer
– see that it is not of your own doing.
It must have been planted in you by a hand
against which you tried your strength in vain,
the invisible hand of the creator
who fashioned you as clay,[14]
who forms and crushes everything according to His will.
What is the point
of confining your deepest longings to the tabernacle
until it falls
so that you desire nothing eternal
except what you know to be impossible
– eternal life in this tabernacle,
which day by day approaches its irrevocable fall?
And can it help you
since you feel that at the same time you are deceiving your heart?
– since you feel at the same time
that what the Word testifies is true:

172

When the tabernacle has fallen
and you never sought nor found a better dwelling-place,
then, as you lie dead and buried,
you will wake up like the rich man
homeless and in torment
and you will see, on the other side of the gulf
in the bosom of Abraham,
the quiet habitation
that you would not heed
and would not win

Oh, man!
Do rather what is better
and listen with devotion to the psalmist
when he sings:
One thing have I asked of the Lord,
that will I seek after;
that I may dwell in the house of the Lord all the days of my life.
to behold the beauty of the Lord,
and to enquire in his temple.[15]
Indeed, my Lord
I shall dwell for ever in thy tabernacle.
Listen to the prophet who cries:
"Look upon Zion, the city of our solemnities:
thine eyes shall see Jerusalem
a quiet habitation,
a tabernacle that shall not be taken down,
whose stakes shall never be removed
and whose cords shall never be broken,[16]
and no inhabitant shall say, I am sick:
for the people that dwell therein
have been forgiven their iniquity"[17]
Learn then to pray,
to raise a song to your Maker:
"O God, send out thy light and thy truth:
that they may lead me,
let them bring me
unto thy holy hill, and to the tabernacles.
Then will I go in unto God,
my exceeding joy:

yea, upon the harp will I praise thee,
O God, my God!"[18]
Say not, what does it avail!
For if you but lift your eyes from the dust
to seek the eternal dwelling-place,
if you but sigh with your heart for it,
sigh that also your eyes may glimpse Zion,
that also for you the gate and the door will be opened
to the court of Heaven
and the sanctuary of the Lord,
then He is standing beside you in Spirit,
the blessed one,
whose countenance is as the dawn of eternity,
the words of whose lips are as dew upon plants,
as life out of death.
Surely you know him,
it is He who looks down
from the lovely rooms at the Father's right hand
and testifies:
"Ask and it shall be given you
Seek and ye shall find
Knock and it shall be opened unto you.[19]
Come unto me,
Come unto me, all ye that labour and are heavy laden,
And I will give you rest
Ye shall find rest unto your souls[20]
For in my Father's house are many mansions,[21]
and where I am there shall my servant also be."
You know him well, O man,
you who were baptized through His word
and in His name.
And if you do not know Him
or have forgotten Him,
then get to know Him,
remember then your Lord
your Master, your friend and Saviour.
Go to Him and be not afraid
when your eye looks for the house of the Lord,
when your heart seeks eternal comfort.
Be not afraid that He will reject you,

for He has vowed
that whoever comes to Him
will never be rejected.
Say not, who shall ascend into heaven
to bring Him down to me",[22]
Say not, where shall we find Him,
for truly He is not far from any of us,
"He is as near to us as the Word
in our mouth and in our heart",[23]
the Word of Faith that we preach,
and He has said:
"I dwell in the high and holy place,
with him also that is of a contrite and humble spirit,
to revive the spirit of the humble
and to revive the heart of the contrite ones".[24]
Search for Him then in the Word alone,
there you will find Him.
Search for Him then in today's text,
there you will find Him by the bier,
by the body of a mother's only-begotten son,
where with a human heart and a spirit divine
He pities and comforts,
says to the widow, Weep not,
says to the dead, Arise,
and is obeyed and praised.[25]
Go to Him, you whose longing
is like a sorrowing widow
whose only son,
whose hope, they carry to the grave.
Go to Him and hear
whether He does not say,
Woman, weep not,
and to your hope, Arise,
and see if it does not raise itself up living,
and sink into the bosom of your longing
and bear forth the praise of Jesus Christ on your tongue,
nay, feel if, through faith in Him,
it does not open up the everlasting dwelling-place to your gaze.

Notes

1. Ps 27.4
2. Ps 84.2
3. Ps 84.10
4. Ps 43.3-4
5. Eccl 3.20
6. Isa 33.20
7. II Cor 1-6
8. Luke 16.19-31
9. Ps 102.3
10. Mt 24.2
11. II Cor 5.1-4
12. Isa 33.20
13. Jonah 4.7
14. Job 10.9
15. Ps 27.4
16. Isa 33.20
17. Isa 33.24
18. Ps 43.3-4
19. Mt 7-8
20. Mt 11.28-29
21. John 14.2
22. Rom 10.6
23. Rom 10.8
24. Isa 57.15
25. Luke 7.12

Sermon on the 16th Sunday in Trinity 1836:
Luke 7:13

Holy Father, Thy word is truth! Thy word is life and spirit – the word of faith which must be heard! Grant, O Father, in the name of Our Lord Jesus, through the Holy Spirit which is sent out by Thee and is given to us as eternal advocate and comforter, that Thy word of grace and loving-kindness, the great 'Weep not!' may day by day increasingly become *Life and Spirit*, the divine and blessed reality for us, until it is perfected in Thy Kingdom, where Thou shalt wipe away all tears from Thy children's eyes and create an everlasting hymn of praise on our lips. In the name of Jesus, Our Father, who art in heaven!

Weep Not!
Truly, my friend, we dwellers in the Vale of Tears never see more clearly the divine distinction between God's World and our own, than when we consider what the very same "Weep Not" is in the mouth of the Lord and what it is in our own. For then we learn what we unfortunately had almost forgotten, that the distinction lies not nearly so much in what the word means and is considered capable of meaning, as in what it actually is and expresses, in what it can do, what it does, and what it achieves; in short, whether it is life and spirit or merely hot air, which whatever it means, good or bad, is still dead and powerless. Thus the word "Weep Not" means the same thing in every mouth in heaven and on earth, but as a merely human utterance it is the emptiest thing imaginable, whereas in God's mouth, it is the richest, the most desirable and the most beneficient word to a sorrowing heart. For when it is spoken by God it cannot fail to assuage the sorrow, but spoken by man of his own accord it has either no effect whatsoever or it does the opposite of what it says, oppressing the heart that needs relieving, and intensifying the weeping it commands to stop.

Truly, my friends, whenever it seems the heart is being comforted and the tears dried by man saying of his own accord, "Weep

Not", or informing us that the words are to be found in St. Luke's Gospel, then this comes either from the grief being feigned and the tears false, so that only an excuse is needed to stop them or because the *weeper* consoled himself with something quite different from this Word, that is, with a hope of having his affliction relieved and his loss replaced which the World does not contain.

When therefore the affliction is such that no human charity can relieve it, or the loss such that no human power can replace it, it is like an only beloved son that a widow has lost, as in today's gospel, or it is just an old and trusted friend. In short, it is part of something that our heart calls irreplaceable, at whose loss it feels alone and abandoned, or it is a fatal illness that tortures us, an internal unrest and despair that so afflicts us that man's "Weep Not" is, on the lips of most people, merely a mockery or an aggravating stupidity. Even if it was on loving lips and spoken with the best of intentions it would only be an expression of impotent sympathy, casting us deeper into grief and opening the flood-gates for more tears.

Indeed, my friends, it comes to this, that when we tell ourselves in our distress "Weep Not", then however reasonable we consider the grounds for consolation to be, far from allaying the sorrow they actually increase it, and far from calming the tears they encourage them.

When on the other hand Almighty God says to a son of man "Weep Not", then we know that that word dries the tears and allays the sorrow, just as we feel certain that as sure as Jesus Christ was God's only begotten son who spoke the word of the Father, so did His "Weep Not" in today's gospel comfort the widow at the loss of her only son. For she felt that He, who is truly better than many sons, had taken it upon Himself to care for her, so that He who bade sorrows cease had joy to bestow on her and promised that it would come at once.

So to those of us who believe in Jesus Christ it is not a question of whether His "Weep Not" can extinguish all our sorrow and give us full compensation for all our losses, for it goes without saying that even if we had lost our only son, then God's only son is a far better support and God's beloved son far more beloved, and furthermore empowered when He sees that our peace and happiness depend on it, to raise from the dead with a word from God, just as He raised the widow of Nain's son and gave him back to his mother. No, the only question for us is whether the Lord really speaks to us, whether He still speaks peace to His children and His saints, whether He still says to the sorrowing hearts of His believers, "Weep Not"; in other words, whether the forgiveness of sins, the resurrection of the body and the life everlasting are as certain for us, as comforting and joyful as they should be when we have His word for them. And since He Himself is the Truth, they can never lie, and since He has all power in heaven and on earth He must put such power into His word that it really is, expresses and does all the good and all the joyful things that it contains and that it means.

Indeed, my friends, our forefathers felt deeply, and so must we all, that the true presence of the Lord amongst us, with His spirit and His word, the Word of Grace and Truth is the only truly great question, the only question of life and death in His house and Church; for on that question depends whether His house is to be a dwelling-place for peace and joy, or to be like a house that has lost its head, its support and its defence, a dwelling-place for fear and grief. On that question depends completely whether His Church is to be a nation with King and clergy, a free and a great nation, or to be, as the Apostle says, the most despicable, the most miserable of all people.[1]. For that is obviously what we would be if we merely placed our hope in the earthly life of Christ that is past, and in the coming of a dead man into the clouds of heaven and for that reason broke with this world and all that is of this world.

But then how is this question to be answered?

According to the Scriptures?

No, not for anything! For we cannot see from the scriptures whether *Jesus* really promised to remain invisible but real for other than His Apostles, and we can say nothing about how far He is with us or not; it is our own experience and only our own experience that can teach us that. For however certain we may be that the Lord was with our fathers, it is still no use whatever if He is not at the same time with us; and on that point our forefathers can tell us nothing. The only thing that an authentic witness of the Lord's presence in days gone by can teach us is that if we can miss the Lord it is not His fault but our own, and even this information would be useless and only of benefit to us if we could discover and correct the error that bereft us of the Lord and all the peace and comfort and joy He alone can pour out in the Word that is life and spirit.

It is our sins, said our forefathers when they felt the absence of the Lord, that make a separation between Him and us, and in a way they could be said to be right; yet this obviously brought them no enlightenment and only obscured all the more the most important question as to how one should seek the Lord so as to find Him. For, admittedly it is our sins that from the very first create a separation between God and us, but the Only-begotten came to the world not to search for the righteous but to call sinners to repentance. It was precisely this that the Pharisees and the Scribes murmured against, that He sought lodging with notorious sinners, associated with and sat at table with them, so that if He is the same Jesus today as yesterday, it cannot possibly be because of our natural sins that He calls us to repentance and, if we have faith in salvation, speaks peace to our soul.

On the contrary! I say now, what I have been saying for a long time: it is not really the fault of our sins, but the fault of our blindness if we miss the Lord's true presence. It can only be the fault of our sins if we with unnatural obstinacy refuse to open our eyes and see him standing amongst us and to open our ears and our heart to the good Word He speaks to us. I say this, that inasmuch as Jesus Christ is God's only begotten Son and inasmuch as the baptism we are baptized with and the Holy Communion we are invited to are instituted by Him, so is He himself also present whereever there is baptism, and where the bread is eaten and the wine drunk in His name and with his Word. It is He Himself that speaks to those who are willing to hear His voice and He Himself who asks, 'Do you believe?" It is He Himself who says to the believer, "I baptize you in the name of the Father and of the Son and of the Holy Sprit." It is He Himself who invites the believers and the baptized to His table and says to them; "Take, eat: this is my body, which is given for you: Drink, all of you, this is the cup of the new testament in my blood which is poured out to you for the forgiveness of sins."[2] It is He Himself, our Lord Jesus Christ, who speaks these words through the lips of his servants whom He has sent out on this mission. And everyone who receives these words and keeps them in his heart as God's Word will learn that they are Life and Spirit, that they have within them the Spirit that quickens, the Holy Spirit that is Christ's true vicar on earth and like the Spirit of Truth, is one with the Lord. The reason why the Lord's presence became steadily weaker and more unrecognisable amongst us and our forefathers was none other than that faith in the means of grace that the Lord has instituted gradually faded and swung over either to the Scriptures and their interpretation, to our prayers and our self-made devotions or to whatever else one cares to name. And the second reason is that those who continued to put their trust in the means of grace concentrated for the most part, not on what was invisible, but on what was visible, not on the Word as it sounds in the mouth of the Lord and as it goes about its work, but on the bodily things that He has joined together through the Word but without which the Word and the Faith in it are simply water and wine and bread and of no benefit. That is why, I maintained, our affliction is now over and our sorrow allayed, for the Lord has opened our eyes to see that He is not far from any one of us, but as close as the Word in our mouth and in our heart, the Word of Faith that truly and explicitly speaks to every one of us so that we have the right to take possession of it and can freely hold it up before him as a pledge that He has promised to redeem with His life and Spirit for ever and ever. It does not depend at all on whether we understand what He means when He says, "I baptize you", and when he invites us to eat His body and drink His blood. It only depends on us believing in Him, giving ourselves up to Him and being willing to do as He says, for when He washed Peter, He said, "What I do thou knowest not now; but thou shalt know hereafter".[3] He demanded only that Peter should believe Him through his Word that if he did not believe in Him, he would have no share in Him. In the same way He demands the faith from us that unless we are reborn in water and spirit we cannot enter into the Kingdom of God, and unless we eat the flesh of the Son of Man and drink His blood, we have no life in ourselves. But if we do so, we shall live with Him as He lives with the Father, and He will raise us up on the last day.

This then is my testimony, and this is why I said so often, and why I repeat, that in the Spirit the Lord has met His church, just as in today's gospel He met the widow with her only son. He has stopped the bier, and said to the Church, our mother, "Weep not". And by raising His Word from the dead through sacraments He has raised the hopes and the consolation of the Church, which is really He Himself, the living word of God.

Whether this testimony is true does not at all depend on my speaking from experience, for it might equally well be a testimony to the Spirit of Truth that the Lord has sent out to His servants to speak through them. But if it is true, then it cannot but move the believers who hear it to seek the Lord where He is to be found, and it follows that He is the same today as yesterday. In the name of Jesus, Amen.

VIII

Poetry

Poetry

Grundtvig's poetical output has no less colossal proportions than his work in other genres. Beside the 1400 hymns there is at least an equally great number of poems with other themes. It goes with this that Grundtvig is the most uneven of poets. This holds true not only as you move from one poem to another, but within the same poem one may find passages of the highest poetic quality side by side with some that are markedly less inspired. That has been a crux for his editors, who seem torn between being faithful to what Grundtvig actually had to say and their concern for showing him as the great poet he truly was.

This poses a problem for the compiler of an anthology of translations, for most renderings of Grundtvig's work are done from pruned versions of the originals; and as often as not translators have also used the knife — one suspects: not so much out of aesthetic concern as because they are defeated by the original text. It has not been Grundtvig's good fortune to find a translator who combines a grasp of his vision with a gift of imagery matching his. That is not to say that there are not worthy attempts at translating his poetry. Quite a few hymns have been done into English by pastors of the Danish Church in the United States. These translations have been made for use in the service, their main concern is to make the texts singable and plain to understand for the congregation. Only in second line comes what Grundtvig actually said and the images by which he expressed it. This tends to make him a more conventional hymn-writer than he really was.

The small selection offered here cannot pretend to give a representative idea of Grundtvig's poetic work. The poems are included to put on record that, with everything else he was, Grundtvig was first and foremost a poet. It is hoped that the five poems may also give an inkling of the subject matter and range of his poetry, and perhaps even of its originality.

The first title is a rendering of the poem "The Land of the

Living" from 1824. At this turning-point of his life Grundtvig weighs the Romanticism of his youth against Christianity as he now sees it. The poem shares its theme with the sermon for 16th Sunday in Trinity 1823 (see above p. 165), man's longing for eternity. In an imagery, indebted to Amos, 9.13, Revelations, 22.5, Isaiah and, possibly, Plato's "Timaeus", Grundtvig describes man's vision of immortality and his fruitless striving to reach it, be it in idealist thought, in poetry or in art. Man's vertical Eros proves powerless. Only the Agape, reaching down from God to man, will open a view to the Land of the Living that is more than a transient glimpse. The second half of the poem shows how the Christian by way of baptism, by faith, hope and charity, will have a share in the Land of the Living, which in this way will stretch from Earth to Heaven. It is evident how Grundtvig's view of man and of God as Love is inspired by his reading of Irenaeus. When in stanza 11 he speaks of the life of the human spirit as kindled by God, he in a way rehabilitates the Romanticism he discards in the first half of the poem: Man harbours a spark of the Divine. In his description of the gulf of death, which faith can cross, Grundtvig in stanza 9 alludes to Norse mythology where there is a bridge from the Land of the Living to the Realm of Death, which crosses a river packed with crashing floes of ice. The use of the word strand may associate one of the Norse names for hell, Nastrond, "the beach of corpses". Grundtvig made another version of the poem with the same beginning as the last stanza here, which brings it more into line with the manner of a church hymn. This version has been translated into English in part by S. D. Rodholm (see below) under the title "Land of Our King".

The poem "The Ages Past ..." (Udrundne er de gamle Dage) was written in 1833 as a devotional song for a non-confessional school in Copenhagen, which catered for both Jewish and Christian pupils. It may be said to reflect the view of man and life Grundtvig had reached in his introduction to Norse Mythology in 1832. Man is recognised as being both mortal clay and eternal spirit. Also, here life is glorified as triumphant over death, as is Grundtvig's view of existence as action and struggle. The poem is among the best loved among those included in the songbook of the people's high schools.

The pentecostal hymn, here selected, describes the loveliness of the Danish landscape at Whitsuntide. With the balmy summer breeze, wafting through the foliage, Grundtvig suggests the descent of the Holy Spirit in the pentecostal miracle, to which the two concluding stanzas are fully devoted. The fusion of image and meaning here is an outstanding example of Grundtvig's masterly application of the poetics of Romanticism to his Christian experience. The hymn was first published in 1853, but it dates from 1843 when the beginning was different. It was Grundtvig's habit to rework and revise what he had written earlier. There are often two or three versions of the same poem.

The hymn was translated by Søren Damgaard Rodholm (1877-1951). He was a pastor of the Danish Lutheran Church in U.S.A. He has with some success translated several hymns by Grundtvig into English.

The poem "Open Letter to My Children" dates from 1839 and is addressed to Grundtvig's children of the first marriage. The original is a longish poem; what is here translated is a section which Grundtvig made into a song that has remained very popular in the people's high schools. The poem gives in poetic form the essence of Grundtvig's ideas about education. The translation is by Johannes Knudsen, one-time Professor of Church History in the Lutheran School of Theology, Chicago. He has contributed several very competent translations of poems by Grundtvig as well as the major monograph on him in English.

The last poem is a translation of Grundtvig's ballad about Niels Ebbesen. He was a Danish squire whose assassination of Count Gerhard of Holstein in 1340 sparked off a revolt against the Holsteiners' domination of Denmark. Grundtvig's source is a ballad of the sixteenth century, but for his version of the story he models himself on the ballad pastiches of the eighteenth century. He has given it a popular appeal, which also comes out in the title-page when it was published in the style of the broadsides of the day. The poem reflects Grundtvig's growing anti-German attitude rooted in his well-founded fear of Prussian aggressive designs against the Dansih border province of Schleswig. The Translation is by Charles Wharton Stock in his anthology A Second Book of Danish Verse (1947).

Niels Lyhne Jensen

The Land of the Living

O, wonderful land,
Where hair turns not grey, falls so softly Time's hand;
Where sun does not burn, nor the seas' white waves fling,
Where autum embraces the flowering Spring,
Where sunset and dawn always glow with the bright
                Noon-radiant light.

O, heavenly land,
Where tears do not run like the hour-glasses sand,
Where wish that is worthy is wished not in vain,
Where lacks only that which here causes us pain.
Of all that we seek for, we long for the most
                Thy halcyon coast.

O, fair promised land,
We hail in the dawn's smiling crystalline strand!
The child takes as real thy bright image there seen,
And dreams thou art found where the forest grows green,
Where children can share with the flowers of May
                Their innocent day.

O, transient dream
Of Eden's green isle in Time's fast-flowing stream,
Of temples of Joy in the Valley of Tears,
Of demigod life in Mortality's spheres.
To most so will vanish to-day as of yore
                The life-giving shore.

Delusory dream!
Thou luminous bubble in Time's flowing stream!
In vain does the bard with his song and his pen
From brilliant shades thee create once again;

When likeness comes nearest, then little ones weep
                    The vision to keep.

                    Enchanting bright dream:
Eternity's pearl in Time's glittering stream!
Thou mock the stretched arms which seek vainly to hold
The hear's dearest wish, so in picture and mould
Men strive to enfold for all time what they know
                    Is destined to go.

                    O, Spirit of Love!
I kiss like a child Thy bright hand which above
From Heaven comes reaching to Earth's heavy mould
And touches our eyelids with fingers of gold,
That heavenlike rises above rumbling strand
                    The wonderful land.

                    O, Name of alle Grace,
Who open to us Thy celestial embrace!
Unblighted the Spirit can touch human clay,
Reviving the leaf that had withered away.
Bowed low to the ground on my knees let me be,
                    But God can me see.

                    O, Faith, Thou most rare!
Whose swaying bridge over the deep can us bear,
Defying the ice-river's loud-roaring strand,
From Death's spectral home to the life-giving land.
Come lower beside me and stay, high-born guest,
                    As you like it best.

                    O, Hope on light wing!
Reborn by the font, my Godbrother, Thou swing
On many swift flights to the land beyond this,
For alle the good tidings Thou brought and this bliss:
When Hope is no longer, then joy I shall see;
                    My thanks be to Thee!

                    O, Love, Thou calm spring,
That feeds the strength flowing within ev'rything!

He calls Thee His Father who will set us free,
All life of the spirit is kindled by Thee;
Thy Kingdom is found where we death overcome,
The Kingdom to come!

Our Father and Lord!
In temples of flesh Thou will best be adored,
As built by the Ghost in the Saviour's Name,
With smouldering altars within human frame.
Such heaven-bright dwellings Thy spark here has won
For Thee and Thy Son.

O, Christian lot!
That gives to the heart what the World has not got.
We understand vaguely, we see now in part,
It lives still within us, we feel in our heart.
For *my* Land, says Life, is on Earth and above,
My Kingdom of Love!

Translated by John Jepson Egglishaw
Revised by Niels Lyhne Jensen

Original: Udrundne er de gamle Dage

The ages past have all flowed by
Like rivers to the Ocean's deep,
And where the weak at last must lie,
The strong man, too, is laid to sleep.
But praise to God, our Lord on High:
The noble kin shall never die.

As graves are dug, the cradles swing,
And Life effaces Death's grim trace.
So north and south the noble bring
Renewal to their proper race.
Down through the ages ever sounds
A witness how God's grace abounds.

So let us keep before the eye
What nobles call their souls' delight,
Yes, let us with the champions vie
And risk with Death itself a fight.
To challenge grave and Death shall be,
So help us God, our victory.

Translated by Niels Lyhne Jensen

Hymn for Whit Sunday

The sun now shines in all its splendor,
The light of life with mercy tender;
Now bright Whitsunday lilies grow
And summer sparkles high and low;
Sweet voices sing of harvest gold
In Jesus' name a thousandfold.

The peaceful nightingales are filling
The summer night with music thrilling,
So all that to the Lord belong
May sleep in peace and wake with song,
May dream anew of paradise
And with God's praise at daylight rise.

It breathes from heaven on the flowers,
It whispers home-like in the bowers,
A balmy breeze comes to our shore
From paradise, now closed no more,
And gently purls the brooklet sweet
Of life's clear water at our feet.

Thus works the Spirit, still descending,
And tongues of fire to mortals lending,
That broken hearts may yet be healed
And truth may be in love revealed
In him who came from yonder land
And has returned to God's right hand.

Awake, ye voices, deep and ringing,
And anthems to the Lord be singing;
Your beauties lend, ye varied tongues.
To praise his name in joyful songs,
And ye, his church, with one accord,
Arise and glorify the Lord.

Translated by Søren D. Rodholm

Open Letter to My Children

A plain and active joyful life on earth,
A treasure ne'er for power or gold to barter,
A guided life, the nobleness of birth
And equal dignity each human's charter,
A life created, tuned to the above,
Alert to man's God-granted gift for living,
Profoundly mindful of the need for love
Which God, the Father's, grace alone is giving.

A life like this I seek for all mankind.
I plan and work a fruitful growth preparing,
And when the seeking wearies out the mind,
The Lord's own pray-er gives me strength and daring.
The comfort of the spirit comes to me
That God has blessed our human, frail endeavour,
That in his hand alone our soul is free
And growth will come in nature's way forever.

A life created, tuned to that above!
A plant is rooted, fed by sun and showers,
The growth which reaps the care of nurture's love
Will find its harvest as a seed from flowers.
And though our day of years be short or long,
Creative growth we may to all be giving.
Our faithful efforts all to God belong,
And sunset glory crowns the gift of living.

Translated by Johannes Knudsen

Niels Ebbesen

There rose a song out of Denmark's grief
Right sad and sore;
There was no native king in Denmark's fief,
But civil war.
The Danes were outlawed in forest and strath,
Rulers we had from heaven's wrath,
When the Germans ran wild in Denmark.

The king who reigned was as fickle of mood
As foam on sand.
Two counts there were of the giant brood
In Holstein land.
Many for plunder and more for deceit,
Foes in the castle and fraud in the street,
When the Germans ran wild in Denmark.

Count Gert was a champion hard and bold
As iron and steel,
And warriors streamed to his castle hold
To serve his will.
All things he risked to gain his end,
Like a nettle he spared neither foe nor friend,
When the Germans ran wild in Denmark.

Count Hans was a chafferer full of guile
With hawk and hound;
Was called the Gentle, for ever a smile
On his lips was found.
Foxes in forest and wolves on the heath,
Rulers we had from heaven's wrath,
When the Germans ran wild in Denmark.

Niels Ebbesen was a knight of fame
In those cruel days,
And ne'er in the Heathland shall his name
Lack a hero's praise.
He quelled that warrior count so high,
Free would he live or free would die,
When the Germans ran wild in Denmark.

The huge count marched to the northern shore
For battle arrayed,
He ravaged the land as he'd done before
With torch and blade.
The Jutlanders all on field or dune
He bade to dance to the Holsteiners' tune,
When the Germans ran wild in Denmark.

"Niels," said Count Gert in the Jutland speech,
"Your time is come,
Unless on the gallows our tongue you'd teach,
Renounce your home!
It will be with you as with all your rabble,
No matter what horses you have in stable,
For the Germans now rule in Denmark."

Niels Ebbesen answered a hasty word:
"Let knaves be hanged,
But hang no knight until good broadsword
Upon shield has clanged!
Mind whom you banish to outlaw's life,
I'll not be far from children and wife,
While the Germans run wild in Denmark."

In wrathful thousands with flaunting boast
The count came on,
Until he had brought his clamorous host
To Randers town;
His evil promises well he kept,
Women trembled and children wept
When the Germans ran wild in Denmark.

Niels Ebbesen came in harness bright
His land to guard,
On an eve in spring he began the fight,
And swords bit hard.
Free would he live and die, he said,
And the giant count on the field lay dead,
When the Germans ran wild in Denmark.

The Holsteiners rallied and came once more,
And our hero fell,
And in many a song on the Jutland shore
His praise they tell.
Still is his glorious memory blest,
For of Danish chieftains he was the best,
When the Germans ran wild in Denmark.

This was five hundred years agone
In joy and woe,
Ere the Dannebrog waved and Denmark shone,
In the evening glow.
The notes of the birds in the forest chime,
And still tell the song of Niels Ebbesen's time.
Let the Germans weep for Denmark!

Translated by Charles Wharton Stork